"Scott's work aims to restore movement, mission, and community transformation to the heart of group life—right where it belongs!"

—Dr. Bill Donahue, PhD, bestselling author,
Leading Life-changing Small Groups

"The practical steps and phases are the genius of this book. You will walk away revisiting your paradigm of missional groups as well as the knowledge necessary to be effective in leading one."

—Rick Howerton, LifeWay

"Boren moves group life back to the place it belongs—in community and on mission. This inspiring and practical book will help you understand the transformational power of God's presence and the agape of his Body to change our neighborhoods. It gives us a glimpse of what our group life can be when we move beyond the chips and salsa in the living room and run into the adventure of following Christ together in the real world."

—Heather Zempel, discipleship pastor,
National Community Church

"Scott Boren is a great thinker and passionate Christ follower. In *Missional Small Groups*, we see those two passions align in a compelling way to serve the church. Scott has written an important book to challenge and help us bring more meaning and purpose to our small groups . . . but not for the purpose you may think. Scott knows the goal of the church is to make not simply better groups but a better world. I am confident we will see both happen as a result of *Missional Small Groups*."

—Bill Willits, author, *Creating Community*;
director of group life, North Point Community Church

"Today, amidst an abundance of small groups literature, *Missional Small Groups* clearly stands out. Boren provides the reader with substantive biblical and theological frameworks for understanding the "rhythms of small groups." These frameworks are insightfully used to inform the lived practices of missional small groups around communing with God, relating to one another, and engaging the world. This is a must-read for anyone interested in living out small group life within the church for the sake of the world."

—Craig Van Gelder, PhD, professor of congregational mission, Luther Seminary, Saint Paul, MN

"Using the concepts Scott Boren presents in this book as the foundation for training and coaching leaders, I am able to cast a greater vision for small groups, groups that go about life together in a way that brings God's kingdom here on earth. The practice lessons he includes will help groups discover and experience what missional small groups are all about."

—Ruth Kelder, ministry developer, Christian Reformed Home Missions

"Scott Boren has experienced and written about small groups for the last twenty years. In *Missional Small Groups,* he breaks new ground by focusing on hearing the voice of God when doing small group ministry and following God's rhythm for the group, rather than the canned model of someone else. This book will stir your creative juices to do small group ministry in a new, dynamic way."

—Joel Comiskey, PhD, president, Joel Comiskey Group

"This is an important book for lead pastors and staff pastors who see their small groups as far more than a key to member retention but don't know how to walk the small group members into a much deeper expression where missional activities happen naturally. If you enjoyed *Introducing the Missional Church* yet finished the book puzzled by how to become more missional, *Missional Small Groups* will provide the practical handles, answers, and first steps you need. I found this book to be a refreshing, energetic read."

—Randall Neighbour, author, *The Naked Truth About Small Group Ministry*; president, TOUCH Outreach Ministries

MISSIONAL
SMALL GROUPS

BECOMING A COMMUNITY
THAT MAKES A DIFFERENCE
IN THE WORLD

M. SCOTT BOREN

BakerBooks

a division of Baker Publishing Group
Grand Rapids, Michigan

© 2010 by Allelon

Published by Baker Books
a division of Baker Publishing Group
P.O. Box 6287, Grand Rapids, MI 49516-6287
www.bakerbooks.com

Printed in the United States of America

Library of Congress Cataloging-in-Publication Data
Boren, M. Scott.
    Missional small groups : becoming a community that makes a difference in the world / M. Scott Boren.
        p.   cm.   —   (Allelon missional series)
    Includes bibliographical references (p.   ).
    ISBN 978-0-8010-7230-7 (pbk.)
    1. Church group work. 2. Small groups—Religious aspects—Christianity. 3. Mission of the church. I. Title.
    BV652.2.B67 2010
    253′.7—dc22   2010001582

10   11   12   13   14   15   16   7   6   5   4   3   2   1

Contents

Series Preface

Allelon is a network of missional church leaders, schools, and para-church organizations that envisions, inspires, engages, resources, trains, and educates leaders for the church and its mission in our culture. Said simply, together we are a movement of missional leaders.

We have a particular burden for people involved in new forms of missional communities (sometimes called "emerging"), people starting new congregations within denominational systems, and people in existing congregations who are working toward missional identity and engagement. Our desire is to encourage, support, coach, and offer companionship for missional leaders as they discern new models of church capable of sustaining a living and faithful witness to the gospel in our contemporary world.

The word *allelon* is a common but overlooked Greek work that is reciprocal in nature. In the New Testament it is most often translated "one another." Christian faith is not an individual matter. Everything in the life of the church is done *allelon* for the sake of the world. A Christian community is shaped by the *allelon* sayings in the Scriptures, a few of which include love one another, pursue one another's good, and build up one another.

As a network of leaders who work with one another, leaders from multiple continents are currently working on a multi-year research project called Mission in Globalizing Culture. Through this project they are asking questions about the formation of leaders in a radically changing context and the demands of a multi-narrative world.

Allelon also collaborates with the Roxburgh Missional Network in its research projects and in providing on-the-ground tools for leaders at all levels of church life. Through its website and consulting and training processes it is furthering the missional conversation in many parts of the world.

In addition, Allelon has partnered with Baker Books and Baker Academic to produce resources that equip the church with the best thinking and practices on missional life. The book you now hold is one of those pieces that contribute to the missional conversation and its practical outworking in local churches. I (Alan) have known and worked off and on with Scott for more than fifteen years. In that time, he has passionately sought ways in which small groups can be effective structures for the formation of people to be what Lesslie Newbigin described as a sign, foretaste, and witness of God's future in Jesus Christ. I have watched Scott wrestle with the big issues around forming missional groups at the heart of local churches. He understands how most small groups have been turned into little more than experiences for individuals and fail to participate in God's great purposes in creation. Scott has worked in local churches to produce something very different. This is not a "how-to-guide" as much as a handbook for leaders wondering how to empower and energize a community seeking to witness to the kingdom in the midst of their lives.

Mark Priddy and Al Roxburgh

Introduction

Some people have rhythm and some don't. I fall into the latter category. I cannot dance very well. I took piano lessons for six years, but today I can't play even one song. I can sing a bit, but the simple act of clapping in rhythm requires so much concentration that I usually have to quit singing in order to clap. For me, being rhythmic only comes through acts of concentrated intentionality.

Thank God he has not made everyone like me. My wife, Shawna, has rhythm. She loves to dance and can do so in ways that add beauty and life to a song. While I may not have it—the two of us on a dance floor is a vision of opposites—I truly enjoy it when I see it. Rhythms rightly done are beautiful things to experience. They create music that draws in the listener and opens up an alternative imagination, a parallel world of hope and beauty.

One such form of music that does this is improvisational jazz. Instead of playing fixed pieces of music, jazz musicians work together to create songs on the fly. The music comes to life as the musicians play off one another and make music in the moment. Improvisational jazz, like life, is lived and experienced, and then it moves on.

In order for jazz musicians to perform this kind of music, however, they must practice. They cannot bank on their natural rhythm and talent. They must learn how to work together, how to read each other, and how to complement each other's strengths and weaknesses. In other words, they must practice the rhythms of jazz in order to make the music of jazz.

In much the same way, we live according to the rhythms we practice. Some are good, and others fail to offer much worth hearing. Most people today play their life rhythms without even thinking about the music their lives make.

About four years ago, my wife and I moved our kids from Texas to Minnesota so I could become one of the pastors who develop small groups at a church in St. Paul. Instead of coming in with a grand plan for how to develop groups, I felt impressed by God to spend a significant amount of time listening to the rhythms of God that were already being played by his people. Much of my energy for the first two years of my job was spent listening, watching, and trying to see what was going on. I must admit that my type-A, get-it-done tendencies made it very hard for me to refrain from introducing a grand scheme, and others also wanted this from me. But the rhythms I heard changed everything.

The following chapters will include stories that reveal these rhythms, but one story in particular helped me enormously. After arriving at Woodland Hills Church, I was told by our senior pastor that I should get to know a man in our church named Kent Garborg. As we met over coffee, Kent told me he was formerly the small groups pastor at another church in the Twin Cities and that he had used much of the material I had written. He had visited many churches that had developed effective group systems and had even met with one of my former colleagues from when I was a groups consultant in an organization in Houston.

At first I was honored that this man of obvious wisdom, experience, and success found what I had written worth using, but then he continued his story. He shared that he and his wife were no longer small group leaders in our church. I was disappointed because here was someone who understood the vision as much as anyone but was no longer part of the leadership.

Instead, Kent had started a weekly ministry with former jail inmates who now lived at the local Salvation Army. He led a thirteen-week introduction to the Christian faith and had organized small groups to process the teaching. Some of the inmates transitioned into a house that his ministry owned. Kent told me about the weekly house church meetings that occurred on Tuesday nights. They shared a meal, confessed sins, read the Scriptures, prayed, and so on.

As he talked, my heart began to race. His story exemplified the kind of thing I envisioned happening through small groups when I first began this journey back in college. But then I realized that for the most part, Kent was doing this alone. He was not connected to any of the ministries or leaders of our church. This man, who was a member of our church and a personal friend of our senior pastor, was doing some of the most kingdom-centered ministry around, but it did not fit into any of our structures. We had all kinds of regular groups that were meeting every week, doing the right group studies, coming to the right leadership meetings, and conforming to the right expectations. They were doing the normal stuff we trained them to do, and I was and am thankful for the impact they have on people's lives. But Kent was doing something outside our training, and the rhythms on the fringe were off our radar screen. It was disturbing.

The more I reflected on Kent's story, the more I was compelled to look at the "normal" small groups that had become the standard fare in churches across North America. What Kent was doing was radically different, and I quickly saw that it was unfeasible for most small groups to take on what he was doing. His story of missional group life could not serve as a model for others to copy, but it caused me to see that we need to invite regular small groups to be more than simply weekly meetings that people attend when it fits their busy schedules. We need to re-envision a way to empower normal groups led by normal group leaders that are full of normal followers of Christ to listen to God and live in such a way that they impact the world around them. The Spirit of God used Kent's story to rattle my cage and open up the door to search for fresh ways to understand how God is using small groups today.

As I reflect on my entry almost two decades ago into group life that aims at being missional, I realize that I longed for a book that would show me what it means to be a group that is more than a *huddle and cuddle* Bible study that is part of my church experience. I, as well as many other group members, expressed the desire for more, but we did not always know what that meant. So often we simply felt guilty that our groups did not live up to our expectations.

Through the years I have found lots of books on small groups—most of which are very good and are written by some of my friends—

that have helped me do groups better. But I have found that most of the time these books simply help me to improve the kind of groups that we already know how to do. In other words, we have been talking about how to play small group music better without ever asking if we are actually playing the *right* music in the first place.

In this process, I began to rethink much of what was being offered through small group conferences, books, and leadership training sessions. I discovered a prevailing general assumption: if people simply join a small group, they will start "playing rhythms" that make a difference in the world. But this is like giving a five-thousand-dollar Gibson guitar to a novice and assuming he or she will suddenly become a studio musician because the novice now has the right instrument. The conversations focused on structures, curriculum, and strategies. The questions seemed to be: How do I lead a small group effectively? How do I get people to attend my meetings? How can I make my group grow? And while such questions are good and normal—I also asked them and even answered some of them myself—they seem to miss the larger questions that really help us play the rhythms that God desires us to play.

As I listened to these new rhythms on the fringe, I began to see that the music does not really fit the music of normal small groups. Therefore, this book takes a different angle to group life and the leadership of groups. Instead of providing a list of ten ways to turn your group from a normal group into a missional group or giving you a litany of technical skills that you need in order to be missional, through this book I seek to reframe your imagination about what small groups are and can be. I invite you on a journey with me of learning to play some new music. The aim of this book is to serve as an introductory music book. The best way to learn to play new music is to play with others, to receive input from a teacher, and to have a good music book to point the way. Therefore, invite others to read this with you, talk about it, and discuss ways to live out these rhythms. Interact with and receive input from a pastor, elder, or coach who can provide spiritual guidance and practical input. If you do this, the words that follow will come to life through your conversations like music through a new band. The sounds might be rough at first, but the practices of doing the rhythms together will begin to come together into a kind of music that changes everything.

12

This book does not provide a program, plan, or method for group success. Instead it points to a way of life together that makes a difference in the world. It reveals ways we can re-engage our neighborhoods with the gospel. Part 1 lays out the difference between normal groups and missional small groups and explains how the music between the two differs. Part 2 then introduces the various practices common to missional groups. Because this is an introductory book on missional group life, some who are farther down the path might find some of what follows to be too elementary. For others who are comfortable in normal small groups, these ideas might be too challenging. As I have shared these ideas over the last couple of years, however, I have found many who are longing to learn to play a new song. As a retired school principal in his seventies shared with me after a daylong seminar, "I came here reluctantly because we have done small groups of all kinds but none worked, and we did not know why. Now I know, and while I can't lead a group anymore, I want to contribute to a group that lives this way."

Deep within God's people, the Spirit is stirring up a longing for more than the normal group experience. Let's learn together how to play the rhythms of missional group life. Or better yet, let's consider how we can join God in his mission in this world.

Part 1

LISTENING

A Different Drum

During my senior year of undergraduate studies, I had an assignment to write a technical training manual. I was the student president of a large campus ministry that had used small groups extensively for the sake of Bible study, accountability, and pastoral care. In this context I had developed as a leader, and it was in the context of small group community that I had learned to receive and give love. So I decided to write a small group manual for student leaders.

When I began doing the research for this manual, I was looking for information on the skills required for leading the kinds of groups that I had experienced throughout my church life. I borrowed a few books from a local church planter, but they did not meet this expectation and instead sent me on a wild ride that has yet to be completed. What I read shocked me because it told of groups that were much more than weekly Bible studies or fellowship groups designed to get people connected. These small groups were made up of people who were committed to live in community with one another in everyday life, and they possessed a call to minister together outside of official meetings. These groups followed the beat of a different drum from the one I had heard in churches. I realized that just going to small group meetings was missing the point. I had to find out how to live in community with others in a way that impacts the world around me.

A Journey of Following Drums

Little did I know how the drumbeat would impact my life. The year after I wrote the manual, I found myself in a top-rate seminary, searching for help in any and every place about how to raise up and train group leaders to live out this kind of community. I looked for small groups in local churches that wanted to touch the world around them and engage in conversations about the gospel and what it means in our world today. Sadly, I was greatly disappointed. I found that most wanted to talk about either traditional forms of church or how small groups might prop up the kind of church we already know how to do.

Then God opened up the opportunity to work on a team with one of the early small group visionaries who had written one of the books that had changed me so. I felt like I was living a dream. I joined a team that promoted a vision for being church and doing small groups that aimed at having an impact upon the surrounding culture. It was not church as usual and it was fun. Most churches were not interested in what we had to say, but almost every day we received a call from a pastor or church leader who confessed his or her longing to do the kind of group life we were promoting. I will never forget the day I answered the phone and a pastor from the Aleutian Islands, located off the coast of mainland Alaska, said, "I have been in ministry for twenty-five years, but in my heart I have longed for something like what you are saying. Thank you."

This small group visionary and others like him constantly played a beautiful beat on a different drum. They cleared a path for small groups that were doing community for the sake of a lost and dying world. Before there was ever any talk about elaborate small group strategies or cell churches or churches of small groups, leaders like Gordon Crosby of the Church of the Savior in Washington DC and Thom Wolf of Church on Brady (now Mosaic) in Los Angeles were empowering mission groups to take the gospel out into life through how they did life together. Each group had a specific mission outside of simply meeting regularly.

18

Ralph W. Neighbour tells stories about his experimental church in west Houston. He tells of groups with executives from large oil companies who would forego sleep to help addicts dry out in a sober house they sponsored. The local bartenders knew that if there was someone in need, they could dial a phone number and someone from a local group would come and help. Another group taught English to Japanese women who moved to Houston with their workaholic husbands. Other groups helped men and women who had lost their jobs to get on their feet during the oil bust of the 1980s when the Houston economy tanked. These were communities on mission even though they did not use that language.

This drumbeat resounded in my heart. And it began to play through my hands and feet in the early 1990s when I belonged to a small experimental church where we tested different ways to do group life and engage our neighborhoods. Small groups were not necessarily our focus; they were simply a mechanism for carrying the kingdom of God to this world. We were a group of nobodies who simply connected with God and each other and sought to share the Good News of Jesus with other people. It was a beautiful missional experience in which we discovered how to show people the life of God in the normal everydayness of our life together. While helping a neighbor move and then sharing a meal, which led to unforced conversations about God and Jesus, I remember feeling like I was living out additional chapters of the book of Acts. I was shocked that the Spirit could use me in regular ways that were so abnormally powerful.

Then something happened. Small groups became popular. Large churches started contacting our ministry and asking us to help them set up small group structures. Up to that point, few had been really interested in what we had to say about small groups. But in the mid-1990s it became part of the church growth mainstream. Small groups became legitimate, and church experts proclaimed that small groups were essential to church health and success. Willow Creek in Chicago, Saddleback in Southern California, and Northpoint in Atlanta became leading voices in the small group conversation. The phones were ringing and the resources were flying out of the mailroom. It felt good.

But in the midst of all of the busyness of helping churches set up small groups, the beat of the drum changed. The original drumbeat called small groups that make a difference in the world was overridden by a new one that unfortunately was identified by the same name—*small groups*. The original drumbeat had produced stories such as a group creating a place in a coffee shop where people could explore Christianity in conversational ways, and groups that adopted a local fire department and befriended the firemen in ways that eventually led to conversational ministry. But when the beat of the drum changed, the stories focused instead on groups that were designed to enfold the Christians who filled the pews on Sunday. I don't think anyone set out to beat that rather normal drum, but how we talked about groups changed nonetheless. There was less emphasis on groups doing out-of-the-box things to impact life in neighborhoods, engage people at the workplace, and empower people in the groups to be missionaries. Instead the focus moved to talk about which was the best curriculum, whether to worship in groups, and if it was realistic to expect people to meet more than once or twice a month. There was a subtle shift from what God was doing through the groups to various techniques to get churched people to join small groups.

Don't get me wrong. I am not wishing that these groups had not developed, because God does use them and moves through them to touch many, including me. But the drumbeat is normal.

Finding the Drumbeat in an Unexpected Song

I had to find the old beat again. I could not quiet the yearning within me with more talk about strategies and tactics to improve my small group leadership. I longed to hear a rhythm that would get inside me, my group, and the groups in our church that might move us into new and unexpected music that would touch those around us who had no interest in coming to church on Sunday. So I listened. At first I wanted to find a list of practical steps for playing this music. I wanted to do something, to make something happen, but that is not what occurred. I needed instead to hear the music from an unexpected song and allow this to get deep within me so that I would never again come close to settling for normal group life. This unexpected song is one called *marriage*.

The Bible refers to the church as God's bride. The Spirit of God is moving to prepare a bride who is ready for the return of the groom. Paul Eddy, teaching pastor at my church, has spent about twenty years researching the biblical theme of covenantal relationships between the bride and the groom, and his teaching has opened my ears again. In the first century the marriage process was much different from how we experience it today. When a man and a woman became what we would call *engaged*, they were entering a *betrothal period*. To be betrothed was a hairline away from being married. In fact, with betrothal, the commitment to marriage was made even though the couple did not live together or have sexual intimacy until after the wedding ceremony.

For about a year the woman prepared herself for her groom. Her friends and family supported her by teaching her what she needed to know to be a faithful bride. The groom went away and, with his family, prepared a physical home for the bride, often attached to his father's dwelling. Neither the bride nor the groom knew the exact date of the wedding; that was determined by the groom's father. When the father decided that his son was ready, he announced the arrival of the wedding day. The groom led his family and friends in a wedding processional to the house of the bride. They then had the official marriage ceremony and finally consummated the one-flesh union as husband and wife.

This understanding of first-century Jewish marriage customs sheds light on some of the things Jesus teaches. For instance, he says,

> Do not let your hearts be troubled. Trust in God; trust also in me. My Father's house has plenty of room; if that were not so, would I have told you that I am going there to prepare a place for you? And if I go and prepare a place for you, I will come back and take you to be with me that you also may be where I am. You know the way to the place where I am going.
>
> John 14:1–4

Jesus invites us to participate in the formation of his bride. We are not yet formally married—that will occur upon his final return. But we are much more than engaged to him; we are betrothed. We are in a time of preparation, a time of learning to live life as the faithful bride. That insight opened my ears to hear a song that is much bigger than leading my group successfully so that people want to attend. I heard a song that is about how we do life, not just what Bible study we use or how many attend each week.

I love the movie *Hoosiers*. Gene Hackman plays coach Norman Dale, who leads a basketball team from a small country high school to the state championship against a large city school. Early in the movie he tells his team of six boys, "Basketball is about five players on the court operating as one." Basketball only works as the team learns to play a rhythm as a unit. The team practices in order to learn how to play together. Basketball does not work if the individuals just do their jobs independently, even if they have unusual talent. They must come together and play together. In much the same way, the preparation of the bride is about practicing together to learn what it means to be Jesus's betrothed. Normal small groups seem to focus on supporting the individuals and helping individuals live in ways that we assume God will bless. But the different drumbeat that was pounding within me called me to live in such a way with others that we become a unit following a beat that is not normal.

This does not come easily to Westerners who have learned to live according to the drumbeat of rugged individualism. We know how to pull our lives together and then contribute to the team effort. And if we don't know how to do this, then we are taught to keep to ourselves and not bother others.

The beautiful thing about playing as a team is the fact that the team owns the weaknesses just as much as the strengths. The Spirit of God is playing a rhythm through community where the personal weaknesses, brokenness, and pain are not things that have to be fixed in order for the community to work but instead are the very things the Spirit redeems and uses to impact our world. We are not called together as a group of top-rate soloists who can impress the world with our talent as great Christians. We are called together as an orchestra comprised of muddled, stumbling rejects who are trying to figure life out like everyone else. Then we simply offer what we have and see what can come of it for the sake of others. The individuals within the church are the bride together. Here we stare fully at the incredible, wonderful mystery of God: he can use what the world sees as weakness for the salvation of creation.

God's Drumbeat

In order to hear God's view of marriage and the relationship between Jesus and his church, we must hear the rhythm of covenant love. Paul Eddy defines it as "a committed agape-love relationship between two or more parties, expressed in specific terms, grounded in promises of faith and faithfulness, that brings blessings of life."[1]

God fulfilled his covenant with his creation when Jesus came, died, was raised, and then sent the Holy Spirit as a down payment on the ultimate fulfillment of our relationship with him. God is a promise maker and a promise fulfiller. His kind of love plays the music of faithful keeping of what he says he will do so that his bride might participate in the blessings of his life.

God's rhythm of covenant-keeping love is not one that hordes what God already has in and of himself. The God revealed in Jesus is a God of wild self-giving and sharing love that frees creation to participate in God's life and love.

As I reflected on my normal small group experience, I realized that we were pretty good at giving love to one another, but we were not participating in the kind of self-giving love through which we open ourselves up to others to share what we had with them. This other drumbeat pointed to a kind of group experience in which group members learn *together* how to be a bride who plays the rhythms of the bridegroom. *Instead of doing groups for the sake of experiencing community, groups experience community for the sake of participating in God's redemption of creation.*

I remember one of the first times I experienced this with a group. It was almost magical, but at the same time it was rather pedestrian. The everyday life was filled with great mystery and awe as we simply committed to being with one another and worked together to share that life with other people. While we were spending time with some non-Christians, one of them said, "You guys actually believe this stuff and you have fun doing it." When we follow this different drumbeat, we manifest to the world the fact that God actually keeps his promises.

Sandra Unger is one of the pastors at our church. About six years ago she was an executive pastor at a large church in Detroit and was ministering to women entrapped by the life of prostitution. She was asking God about how he would address the needs of the poor whom she was meeting. She sensed God say to her, *Through my people.* He longs to play this drum through his people.

God has called his church to form communities that seek to live faithfully as the bride of Christ by sharing what they have with others who don't. By doing so, we are being formed by the Spirit for the ultimate return of the bridegroom. As I continue to listen to this unexpected song of marriage, the call to missional small groups goes deeper and deeper into my very being. I realize that the missional group song is not simply about getting people saved, growing my group, or doing service projects for people in need. This song invites me into a new way of seeing life and, for that matter, the church.

Talking about the Rhythms We Hear

I wish God had given us a manual that explains clearly and succinctly the exact steps I need to take to lead great missional small groups that express faithfully what it means to be the bride of Christ. I truly wish I could write a book that outlines five patterns of missional small groups or eight principles of missional life together and then provides the worksheets, study guides, and manuals for getting this done. But this is not the way we learn to play the music of missional groups, and it seems to me it is not the way we learn the best things in life either.

My sister and I took piano lessons for six years. We had the same teacher who used the same steps and much of the same music. But my sister can play the piano today and I can barely find middle C. It is not that I don't like music or that I did not want to play the piano. The difference is that the steps followed by our teacher fit my sister's learning style and did not fit mine at all. She followed a one-size-fits-all teaching approach, and it failed to teach me much of anything no matter how hard I worked at it.

If we are going to learn the rhythms of group life, we begin not with one-size-fits-all how-tos but with listening to one another and creating conversations about what it means to be God's people on mission in this world. In *Introducing the Missional Church*, Alan Roxburgh and I point out three conversation topics that help shape the life of a missional community today. The first is the reality that we live in a time in the West during which we have to be missionaries in our own land. We can no longer think in terms of church as usual at home and doing missions oversees. Our context demands that we listen to what people are saying, and for the most part, the average person in our culture cares very little what is going on in our churches, how good our preachers are, or how effective our small groups are. Chapter 2 explores this topic and applies it to the small group life.

The second conversation topic revolves around what it means to be the church and how the people of God should be a sign, witness, and foretaste of God's dream for the world. As has been stated in this chapter, throughout history God has worked through a specific group of people, calling them to manifest his life to the people around them. Chapter 3 looks at four ways that small groups have either contributed to or fallen short of this dream.

The third conversation topic is about God, the gospel of Jesus, and what God is doing in this world.[2] This conversation helps us develop the ability to recognize what the Spirit of God is doing in the world and through us as God's people. It gives us the ability to see how small groups can be more than a support system for church as we know it or as a method for resurrecting a dying church system. This conversation leads us into dialogue with the world around us so that we see how the Good News of Jesus is transforming us to be God's people in new and fresh ways. Chapter 4 looks at how God is working to change us and lead us into missional group life.

As you converse about these topics, you can discover together how you can learn the new missional rhythms in ways that fit your context, your church tradition, and the people around you.

Rhythms of Everyday Life

One of my favorite movies is *Cast Away*, starring Tom Hanks. He plays Chuck Noland, an executive for Federal Express, who is alone on an island after a plane crash in the South Pacific. I was fascinated by Tom Hanks's ability to hold my attention as he tries to deal with his loneliness by conversing with Wilson, the volleyball that becomes his imaginary friend. One of the deep messages of the film is that Chuck Noland's loneliness on the island is just a slightly different form of the loneliness he experienced before being marooned. As an executive who works for an organization that is based on speed of service, he adopted a certain set of rhythms that were dominated by the clock and his pager. This is emphasized in one of the first scenes after he crawls up on the beach. He opens his watch to find that it no longer works and then shakes water out of his pager. His most consistent guides for life are now worthless.

The loneliness of the island is only a physical representation of a loneliness with which Chuck Noland was already very familiar. His story serves as a parable to help us understand our context and see what it means to be a missionary in our own neighborhoods. While we may not be marooned on an island, totally alone and longing for conversation, the average person in North America has more in common with Chuck's experience than we might realize. His is the story of the isolation that consumes our lives and the deep need we have to connect with others.

If we are to understand what it means to be *missional* and be a community that makes a difference today, we need to do much more than simply talk about what missional small groups are and do. It is easy to set up some kind of ideal vision for community that does radical things and then list how-tos so that groups can fulfill the ideal. But more often than not, most groups will simply talk about the vision and not see why it fails to come to fruition. We don't begin a conversation about missional small groups with a picture of what an ideal missional community might look like. Instead, the place to begin is to understand how we live life today in the culture in which we live. We must grapple with what it means for people to do life, not in an ideal way, but in an everyday, real way. When we understand the rhythms of normal, everyday life that most of us live, then we can begin to see how the rhythms of Christ's bride begin to intersect with the rhythms of the culture. To do this, we must listen to the culture with the ears of a missionary.

The Ears of a Missionary

In order to gain a different perspective on the way we actually experience community, it is often helpful to imagine you are listening to how we live life today with the ears of someone outside our modern culture. As an insider it is hard to hear the rhythms we accept as normal. Imagine you are a missionary who moves to North America from somewhere like Brazil or India. Your first assignment is to understand how regular people live in the neighborhood where you live. In other words, you are asking about the life not of those who make the news in Hollywood or Washington DC but of average people who live average lives. Take a few minutes to think about the normal patterns of people who live around you; then write down a few words to describe how we typically do life today.

After leading this exercise countless times, I have found that the lists look very similar. People shout out words like: *overwhelmed*, *busy*, *frenetic*, *stressed*, *isolated*, *lonely*, *overentertained*, *overcommitted*, *technologically based*, *rootless*, *relationally shallow*, *fearful*, and *transient*. The words they use tell a story and interpret Chuck Noland's FedEx life in everyday terms that most of us understand. Almost every time someone will say, "Is there anything positive?" Then we come up with words like: *comfortable*, *creative*, *endless opportunities*, *immediate gratification*, *results-oriented*, and *medical advancements*.

Human beings are born into specific social settings that already operate according to a set of rhythms. These rhythms are played by parents, family members, friends, and so forth. And as they play the music of this way of doing life, we learn how to play similar music. For instance, I grew up on a farm where my father woke up early and often worked into the night. I never saw this as workaholism, however, because I got to work alongside him and there was a relaxed pattern to how we worked together. Therefore, I highly value the rhythm of hard work and a productive day. But there are many of my friends whose fathers worked just as many hours but at an office. They have a totally different attitude toward their fathers and a quite different perspective on work. While the rhythms might look similar, they are subtly different in very significant ways.

Rarely do we question the rhythms that these social settings teach us. For instance, we accept the customs of those who raised us (parents, grandparents, and so on), many times assuming what we learned from them is the only *right* way to do things. We operate within the rules of these rhythms even though they are most often created by powers that do not belong to the kingdom of God.

These rhythms are simply part of the culture in which we live. Culture can be basically described as "the sum total of ways of living built up by a human community and transmitted from one generation to another."[1] Culture is made up of the unspoken and assumed ways of life that penetrate all that a social system is and does, and it is passed on to subsequent generations without having to specifically identify what they are and how to live them. Culture is absorbed, and like an accent, you don't realize how culture works or that it is even present until you are exposed to other cultures.

Our Personal Rhythms

In order to map out some specific rhythms that dominate our culture, Randy Frazee, in his book *Making Room for Life,* provides some insightful direction. Imagine Pat—a busy man who works hard as a subcontractor, building cabinetry for new homes. It is common for his days to extend until after dark because his job takes him all over the metroplex. He needs the extra money from taking on more jobs, but it causes stress for him because he often misses dinner with the family. Actually, the kids he lives with are not his. John and Jenny, busy teenagers who are working hard in high school to qualify for athletic scholarships, are the children of his second wife. He has one son of his own in college and a daughter who is twelve and has a learning disability. He has not lived with either of them since the divorce from his first wife ten years ago. On the side, Pat is a volunteer fireman—something he loves because he can serve the community and connect with other service-minded people. He lives to fish, but he spends more time fixing his boat than actually using it. His wife is no less busy. She has four siblings who require quite a bit of emotional energy because of family strife, and she is the primary caretaker of her parents, who are not well. She does all of this while serving as the customer service manager for a large department store chain.

Pat appears to have a good life. They seem to be doing all the right stuff to be successful. To most, they may even seem happy. But when you look at the way they live their everyday lives, it quickly becomes clear that they are playing rhythms that shape their lives, some for good and some not. We can use the Life Rhythms Diagram to illustrate how Pat does life. (See figure 1.)

All of the circles around Pat illustrate the different parts of his life that he must manage. He has a lot of people in his life, but no relationships of any depth. In fact, he has so many circles that all of his time is consumed with managing surface relationships; he has no time for deep, committed friendships. He even struggles to find time to be with his wife. Randy Frazee calls this "crowded loneliness."[2] This is a dominant rhythm of life in the world today, and most don't even question it. It is just the song that we sing, and we join in on the music because most of us know how to play it quite well.

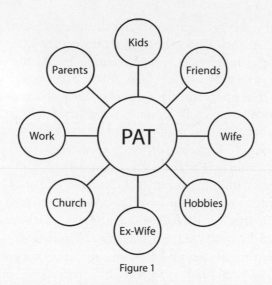

Figure 1

Then if you add to this the fact that the average person in North America watches over twenty-eight hours of television per week, moves every four years, and typically knows more intimate details about people in Hollywood than about their own neighbors, the rhythms of our society revolve around the isolated individualist who is forced to make it on his or her own.

We were made to play a different kind of rhythm—the *connection rhythm*. Just as our bodies are designed to consume food and water in certain proportions in order to maintain health, so are we hardwired for social connections in order to live healthy lives. Chuck Noland realized this in our *Cast Away* parable. On that island, he longed to connect. He felt the need for conversation. He wanted to feel the presence of another. The time on the island depicts Chuck having extensive conversations with Wilson, a volleyball with a face painted on it with his own blood. After four years Chuck manages to build a raft and venture out into the open sea, hoping for rescue. He straps Wilson securely for the ride and heads out. But Wilson comes loose during a storm, falls over the side, and floats away before Chuck realizes what has happened. As the raft and ball drift in different directions, Chuck writhes over the lost ball. When I watch this scene, I cannot help but feel the agony of losing a conversation partner.

31

The social systems of our world are designed around a certain set of rhythms that work against how we were wired as a part of creation. After creating Adam from the dust of the earth, God said, "It is not good for the man to be alone" (Gen. 2:18). Then he created Eve as a companion. The interesting thing about this passage is the fact that Adam was not completely alone. God was present in the Garden of Eden in a way that no man or woman has experienced since sin entered the world. Adam walked with God in daily fellowship, and he tended the animals. But there was no one like Adam—no one who could connect with him on his level. Because of this, he was alone. Every man and woman in the world needs companions who connect on the level of true knowledge of one another. Without this kind of knowledge and connection, we are isolated and alone.

In our culture it is easy to be driven by expectations to produce. But if man had been made only for work, Eve would not have been necessary. We will never be satisfied unless we are connected to others in this life because we are made in the image of God, who is the model of perfect relationality. God is Father, Son, and Spirit—three persons who are eternally one in being and in relationship. First John 4:16 states, "God is love." This is true not because of feelings or even because he must be this way. It is true because it is. Love is what makes God *God* because love is what connects Father, Son, and Holy Spirit as an eternal unit of relationships. God is first of all relational, and from this relationality flows his life and actions.

The Social Brain

Love is the song we play when we are our best selves. We cannot avoid it. As beings formed in God's likeness, we are most ourselves when we live in relationality. When I consider the times when my life has been the most fulfilling, it was times spent with trusted friends playing card games, sharing a meal, or just sitting and talking. It was the times when someone invested in my life as a mentor and I in turn invested in others.

Recent research has confirmed this through the emerging development of the field called "social neuroscience." Over the last ten years psychologists and neuroscientists have performed research not just upon individuals but on the impact of individuals as they interact with others. Through this research they have found what they label the "social brain." In his book *Social Intelligence*, Daniel Goleman writes,

> The social brain is the sum of the neural mechanisms that orchestrate our interactions as well as our thoughts and feelings about people and our relationships. The most telling news here may be that the social brain represents the only biological system in our bodies that continually attunes us to, and in turn becomes influenced by, the internal state of people we're with.[3]

In other words, this is the only biological system that responds to stimuli external to the skin. All other systems are internally responsive. But this part of our brain allows us to have *brain-to-brain* connections with others and thereby influence others through our facial expressions, voice inflections, acts of kindness, and words of affirmation or condemnation. Our expressions of love or lack thereof have a biological impact upon others. As a result, the kind of relationships we practice will shape the way our brain works, whether positively or negatively. Our relationships shape us biologically because every part of us is hardwired to be in relationships with others.

Goleman writes, "Among people around the world, nourishing relationships are the single most universally agreed-upon feature of the good life. While the specifics vary from culture to culture, all people everywhere deem warm connections with others to be the core feature of 'optimal human existence.' "[4] If the relational rhythms we practice directly impact our body chemistry, it might be wise to develop rhythms that line up with the way our body is designed to work.

Being Missional Is Being Relational

Being missional is often viewed as doing a set of tasks to minister to people outside the church. Many interpret it as simply turning from an internal focus to an external focus. So some assume a missional person will do a certain set of missional activities—usually in the form of sharing an evangelistic message with others, engaging in personal evangelism, promoting social justice, or doing nice things for the poor. Groups assume that they are being missional if they serve food periodically at the homeless shelter or pass out meals to the needy at Thanksgiving.

Helping the lost or the poor, while good, is not what I mean by being missional. Service projects are good; feeding the poor, packing lunches for the homeless, and sharing our faith are noble tasks. But God's missional rhythms run much deeper than a list of tasks we can check off. In our context, if we are going to be missionaries in a culture that plays the rhythms of the FedEx life, then we must learn to be relational in the way we interact with one another and in our neighborhoods. Too easily we turn being missional into a project in which those of us inside the church perform some action for those outside the church.

The words of Saint John of the Cross from the sixteenth century help us to see why missional and relational go together. He says, "Mission is putting love where love is not." First of all, it is about "putting love where love is not" in the midst of others who do not have love. We can do all kinds of good things such as giving money, donating to the food pantry, investing personally in building projects; we can talk about what we are doing as a church for those in need; but none of this means that we actually love. To love means being in relationship with others who do not have that love. We are investing in them not just through projects but through continued, often very costly interaction.

Second, "putting love where love is not" is much larger than trying to get people to say a prayer or come to church. When we enter into relationship with others in love, we don't come with hidden agendas or, as a participant said in one of my seminars, "with our Bible up our sleeve." To be on mission is to live the rhythms of God's love with those who don't have it. As Saint Francis of Assisi said, "Preach the gospel at all times—if necessary, use words." Of course we share the message of Jesus's life, death, and resurrection. Of course we invite people to follow Jesus. But "putting love where love is not" is about who we are and the rhythms of life that we play.

Third, "putting love where love is not" is about *being* love. This means we must actually be a people of love in order to take love on mission. I have encountered too many groups who want to *perform* some kind of missional act for God and impact the world, but they don't see the need to *embody* the kind of love that will actually impact the world. Being relational and being missional are intricately connected. We cannot divide the two. The church has nothing to offer the world if it does not embody the message of Good News that it aims to share.

3

Listening to Your Small Group Story

Some of the most memorable songs are those that tell a story. Think of songs like "Imagine," by John Lennon, "My Heart Will Go On," by Celine Dion, and "Lady," by Kenny Rogers. Elton John's "Candle in the Wind" was originally a story about Marilyn Monroe, and it became famous again when he rewrote it into a tribute about the life of Princess Diana. In just a few minutes, great songs draw us into storied rhythms that take us into another world and generate a new imagination that sticks with us.

In order for musical storytelling to work, the rhythm of the music must match the message of the song. To use an upbeat rhythm to sing a song about the loss of a spouse just won't work. The rhythms are part of the story; the rhythms actually shape how we hear the song.

Over the last twenty years I have had the opportunity to listen to small group rhythms in various forms. As a small group member and leader, I have experienced some rhythms that created songs I like, others that were less than memorable, and still others that were painful. As a pastor, I have tried to figure out why some groups have rhythm and others don't. As a researcher and consultant, I have tried to understand why some churches know how to play the song of small group community while others just muddle along.

About a year ago I was thinking back through my small group experiences and what I had assumed were the things that produced good music. I had taught leaders how to use the right curriculum, how to structure group meetings, and how to properly apply the Scriptures. I had written about the proper ways to use icebreakers, what makes a good Bible discussion, and how to grow groups. All kinds of technical things about small groups came to mind, but none of these things actually sounded very melodic to me. In fact, as I reflected back on my best small group experiences, many times—if not most—we did some, if not many, of these technical things wrong.

Then I thought about what did change my life, what motivated me to be different, and what caused me to practice a life that made a difference in the world. In each of these group experiences, a specific story came to mind. I remembered sharing a meal, laughing about life, crying about a tragedy, sharing a need, or experiencing a special time of meeting with God. I remembered our group ministering to a neighbor through a time of cancer and leading her to Jesus. I remember helping someone in need move. I remember simply sitting around talking with someone into the wee hours of the night. Like a great song, I could not get these stories out of my head, and somehow they became part of me without my even knowing how.

As though I was struck by a lightning bolt, I suddenly realized that every small group tells a musical story—one shaped by a set of rhythms. Some of my stories are awesome and memorable, and they spread throughout my being like a virus that brings healing. I will never forget my first such experience. While driving to a meeting I was to lead, I sensed God guiding me to say nothing that night but instead to open it up for whatever people wanted to talk about. That night we played a new song as people opened up about their past and their current reality. Our song told a story about freedom, acceptance, and what it means to live differently in the world.

While reflecting on the various stories I know from small groups and the various rhythms that produced them, I recognized four different stories within small group life. Groups typically play rhythms that tell one of these four stories:

1. The Story of Personal Improvement
2. The Story of Lifestyle Adjustment

3. The Story of Relational Revision
4. The Story of Missional Re-creation

These stories help us understand how missional groups are distinct from the normal groups that are so predominant in our churches today. The stories are connected to the life rhythms we play in our culture, which we identified in the last chapter. As we look into these stories, we will see how Pat is affected as the rhythms played by the group change. The first two stories are taken from normal small groups that seem to operate relatively easily in our fast-paced culture of the FedEx life, while the last two invite us into a way of living that stands in contrast to the patterns of our culture. These last two stories help us grasp what it means to live in missional community.

The Story of Personal Improvement

Small groups that live out this story play rhythms that sound something like this:

> We get together because life is tough in this world and we need a few friends. It is not always convenient for us to meet every week, but we do meet when we can. Usually we meet in short six- or seven-week periods or we meet a couple times a month. We get together, talk a bit about God or study the Bible, and share what is going on at work and in our family. I am not sure that we are close, but it is good to have a place where we can share a little about what is going on in our lives. Being in my small group has improved my life.

This kind of group provides an opportunity for people to improve the normal rhythms of their normal lives. For instance, Pat might attend a small group because it is a place that helps him manage the circles in his Life Rhythms Diagram a little better (see page 31). Little or even nothing about the rhythms of Pat's life changes except the fact that he attends a small group when it is convenient.

In this story, the focus lies on whether the group is beneficial to Pat's life. Pat attends if he likes the people, if the group leader is competent, and if the material is about a topic in which Pat is interested. Such group experiences are often better than nothing. People feel supported, taste a sip of love, or learn a bit about the Bible. But this is far from the only story about small group life.

The Story of Lifestyle Adjustment

The rhythms played by a small group in this story sound like this:

> This group has become a priority to us. We have adjusted our schedules to meet together at least every other week, but usually we meet weekly. In our meetings, we either study the sermon preached by our pastor or use a Bible study guide that we all find personally beneficial. We truly enjoy each other's presence, and we put a high priority on the group and the members in the group. We even do something social once each month. We rise to the occasion when someone has a need, and there is a sense that we are friends.

When Pat enters this story, it requires some adjustment to the Life Rhythms Diagram. Group life is not just added on top of all the other stuff Pat does. Room has been made in his weekly schedule for this group of people because the meeting is a priority and the group members have become friends. There is usually a range of adjustment here. Some might simply choose to not work overtime so they can get to the group meeting on time, while others plan a social outing or host the meeting. Usually the biggest change in this Lifestyle Adjustment story is a change in social priorities.

While the Improvement story is about convenience, the Adjustment story is usually about commitment to formal gatherings. The group members have committed to playing rhythms that focus on attending weekly meetings and other scheduled group events.

In my experience, most small groups in North American churches are living the Adjustment story. For the most part, the people in those groups are living lives that are an adjustment from the predominant life of the wider culture. In other words, the group experience is simply laid on top of the typical American way of life. Church leaders know how to establish group systems, small group leaders know how to lead good group meetings, and group members know how to participate in group discussions. But the general rhythms of life look a lot like the general rhythms of most of the people who don't

40

attend the groups or church. And I have yet to find many who will admit satisfaction with this story. God has planted his Spirit within us that causes us to yearn for more.

The Story of Relational Revision

When a group of people play the rhythms of this story, the song has a distinctive sound:

> Our group has a weekly meeting, but I am not sure that you would call it a *meeting* in a formal sense of the word. When we get together, it is the culmination of the rest of the week when we have been *in* one another's lives. It is a time of sharing what God has been doing, praying for each other, and talking about how God is using us in our normal lives. Yes, we do have a weekly lesson, but the leader usually only asks one or two questions from it.
>
> The most important part of our group, however, is not the meeting; it is how we are connected the other six days. I have never been part of a group in which people are so willing to sacrifice time and energy for each other. And this connectedness actually spills out into our neighborhood. It seems like we are always interacting with, praying for, and serving people who live near us. And in some ways, they are just as much part of our group as those of us who call ourselves *Christians*.
>
> I am not sure how I was able to do life before having this group. This might sound a bit utopian, but it is far from it. Sometimes it is hard. Recently we have had to wrestle with some relational conflict and hurt feelings. In the past I would have run away from such encounters, but not this time. It was not easy, but we pressed through. We are still learning what it means to be God's family.

The basic element to this story is that a group of people is intentionally learning to do life together differently. They are a learning community who know they have not arrived and that they must intentionally practice what it means to be a community that is distinctively Christian and experiences the love spoken of by Saint John of the Cross. They know that they have a mission of "putting love where love is not" and that they must develop rhythms of love that mark them as different from the rhythms of the world.

When Pat begins to live out this story, much more happens than a simple rearrangement of circles. Actually, the way the diagram

41

is constructed begins to change. Instead of Pat as an individual being at the center, Pat becomes part of a community and begins to do life out of a different center—a set of relationships with five to twelve people. But even more importantly, the focus of these people revolves around the presence of Jesus in their midst, moving in and through them as a group. The group has chosen to do community with one another by making the presence of Christ central. If we were to redraw Pat's rhythm diagram, it might look something like Figure 2.

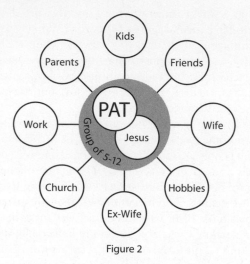

Figure 2

You might notice that there are still quite a few circles in Pat's life. The real world still exists, and Pat has to deal with real stuff. But with the group at the center instead of Pat alone at the center, opportunities are created for some overlapping of circles. Practically speaking, this means Pat's wife does not have to deal with ailing parents alone anymore. The group knows them and has helped to provide food for them, and one person has even stayed overnight at the hospital so that Pat could get some sleep.

The Story of Missional Re-creation

The rhythms of this story stand in stark contrast to the predominant story of our culture. It might sound something like this:

We have developed a way of connecting with each other and God that has resulted in some rather unpredictable developments. Two couples and a single person in our group live within walking distance of each other. So as a group we decided to adopt their neighborhood. We started with a block party. At first it was hard because no one knew us, but after the first party, we started becoming a presence in the community. Then one person started a summer children's Bible study, and as she got to know the neighbors and their needs, we began to pray. Now we have come around a single mom who has three kids, and we include her as much as we can in the life of the group. She has yet to fully understand who Jesus is, but we feel led to embrace her and the kids and see what God does in her life.

Some see the potential to reach people in the community through groups in this story and want a list of things to do so they can join in. But it does not work that way. In the Relational Revision story, a group develops rhythms over time that allow for this kind of dynamic creativity. The hard part of talking about the Missional Re-creation story is the fact that when groups play these rhythms, the actual manifestations of them are always different. There is no singular form or function for what a group might look like here. Some groups might look just like most other small groups except that they are being used in very creative ways to engage their neighborhood. Others might establish a house church that looks nothing like typical small groups, like the story of Kent Garborg I told in the introduction.

Pat and his wife moved into an economically underresourced area and began to get to know people on their street. They invited neighbors to share life around meals and around his car-repair abilities. As Pat and his wife got to know neighbors, they started facilitating an annual block party. In addition, they were friends with another couple who planned to relocate after retirement, and they shared with them their desire to bring the gospel to this street. This retired couple bought a house a few doors down. At this point, the missional small group is not simply about meetings and Bible studies. It is about seeing what God wants to do in the neighborhood. This "Pat" story is actually based on a group that meets in Saint Paul. One day a couple of years ago, one of their neighbors was being evicted. She was an eighty-year-old retired schoolteacher who was an atheist. Within hours the neighbors who had been developed by these two couples made a few phone calls and got her moved and set up. This atheist would never darken the doors of our church, but she got a taste of the gospel that day.

To help groups enter into this kind of life, two questions can be asked:

1. What gifts does this community possess that might be a blessing to the wider community?
2. What needs are found in the wider community that we might meet?[1]

When groups start asking this and engaging people in their neighborhoods, the gospel comes to life and the rhythms of the kingdom begin to create something spontaneous, unexpected, and unpredictable.

Listening to These Stories

When I talk about these four stories with various groups and leaders, I usually get one of three responses:

1. Thank you for being honest with me about what really makes a difference in small group life. We have done groups off and on and tried all kinds of different ways, but we never moved beyond Lifestyle Adjustment. We expected to have a radical impact on our church and community simply because we did small groups. Now we know why our experience did not live up to our expectations.
2. Of course, these last two stories are exactly what I want in group life. Why would I want to be part of a group that does what you describe in the first two stories? In fact, I wish you were more radical and critical of normal groups.
3. What you are talking about is radically different and frankly unattainable by my group. If this is what it means to live in missional community, I am not sure we will ever do it.

Maybe your response is similar to one of these. To be quite honest, I felt all three of these emotions as I thought through these four stories. Recently I was leading a seminar on the four stories, and while we were processing the nature of life in missonal groups, a woman said, "We just don't live that way today." My response was, "That's exactly the point."

Most people live according to the rhythms that have been shaped by the broader culture. Even in our churches this is the case, although most of us don't want to think that we live like those who don't know Jesus. But the reality is that churched people work just as many hours per week, watch just as much television, spend their money in similar ways, and have just as many family struggles as the unchurched.

So if you are like me, your response to these stories might very well be a mixed bag. But I want to ask the questions that the Lord has continually asked me as I have worked through these stories: If we don't live in a way that is distinctive from our culture, then why not? If we are going to be satisfied with living our lives like the rest of the world and adding a weekly sermon and a small group Bible study on top, then what exactly are we up to in the church? Isn't there more? And while the last two stories of Relational Revision and Missional Re-creation might sound different, foreign, and radical, are they really that much different from the foreign ways that Jesus described the kingdom of God two thousand years ago?

Jesus said,

> You are the salt of the earth. But if the salt loses its saltiness, how can it be made salty again? It is no longer good for anything, except to be thrown out and trampled underfoot. You are the light of the world. A city on a hill cannot be hidden. Neither do people light a lamp and put it under a bowl. Instead they put it on its stand, and it gives light to everyone in the house. In the same way, let your light shine before others, that they may see your good deeds and praise your Father in heaven.
>
> Matthew 5:13–16

I find it interesting that Jesus told his disciples, "You are salt, . . . light . . . a city on a hill." He did not say, "You should be . . . ," "You would be if . . . ," or "You could be if . . ." He declared who they were and equipped them to live in a way that fit this declaration.

He does the same for us today. God has put his Spirit within us and given us a new nature. He invites us to learn his ways and discover what it means to live in a way that lines up with whom he made us to be. The words of Jean Vanier from his classic book *Community and Growth* speak to how Jesus is shaping his disciples for community and mission.

> Jesus first of all called men and women to him and told them: "Leave all: come and follow me." He chose them, loved them and invited them to become his friends. That is how it all began, in a personal relationship with Jesus, a communion with him.
>
> Then he brought together the twelve he had called to become his friends; they started to live together in community. Obviously it was not always easy. They quickly began to quarrel, fighting over who should be first. Community life revealed all sorts of jealousies and fears in them.
>
> Then Jesus sent them off to accomplish a mission: to announce good news to the poor, to heal the sick, to liberate by casting out demons. He did not keep them with him for long, but sent them out so that they would have an experience of life flowing out from them: an experience of giving life to people and an experience of their own beauty and capacities if they followed him and let his power act in and through them.
>
> The pains of community are situated between the joy of this communion and friendship with Jesus and the joy of giving life to others: the mission.
>
> If people come together to care for each other, it is because they feel more or less clearly that as a group they have a mission. They have been called together by God and have a message of love to transmit to others.
>
> When two or three come together in his name, Jesus is present. Community is a sign of this presence: it is a sign of the Church. Many people who believe in Jesus are in some degree of distress: battered wives, people in mental hospitals, those who live alone because they are too fragile to live with others. All these people can put their trust in Jesus. Their suffering is a sign of the cross, a sign of a suffering Church. But a community which prays and loves is a sign of the resurrection. That is its mission.[2]

4

Relearning the Gospel Rhythms

I grew up around gospel music. Three times a week the rhythms of hymns and Southern Gospel music rang out from our little country church that had been built in 1908. In addition to the songs we sang, another gospel rhythm rang out from our church. The basic rhythm or pattern of how we performed the gospel with our lives was primarily shaped by whether we attended the four church meetings each week. Sunday school, Sunday morning service, Sunday night service, and Wednesday night Bible study formed the basic pattern of our gospel rhythm. Because they were so central to our life, the unstated goal was to get other people to come to church meetings, which were the primary places where the gospel was shared and lived.

Through the years, small groups have been used to support and reinforce this rhythm of church life. Improvement and Adjustment groups have been developed in churches in order to connect people who attend the Sunday services and to help them contribute to the goal of getting more people to attend the Sunday services.

After reading the last chapter, you might conclude that I only value the stories of Revision and Re-creation. You might think that since this is a book about missional small groups that I see no value in groups that are not missional because the stories of Improvement and Adjustment pale in comparison. While I believe that God's view of community looks more like Missional Re-creation, in which small groups of people are seeking God together about how they can live in radical ways to impact their world, we must deal with reality, and this means facing the fact that the lives of most people, including most Christians, are shaped by the FedEx culture we discussed in chapter 2. And if this is the case, then simply proposing a radical ideal for what missional community might look like will only be a pipe dream for most of us.

If we take our context seriously, then we must admit that doing life in missional small groups will be more like a journey than a destination. And on this journey God meets us with the gospel—the Good News that God incarnate took on flesh and came and dwelt in our midst; the Good News that God the Holy Spirit lives in the midst of our current realities and seeks to change us in the midst of them; the Good News that God the Father passionately loves us and invites us on a radical journey to be transformed from the inside out. Moving into missional life in small groups is about hearing the rhythms of the gospel again and relearning what the gospel means in our daily lives, not just when we attend church meetings.

Settling for a Limited Gospel

Imagine a friend dropped you off at the airport and you checked your bags, secured your ticket, and passed through the security check. Then you walked up and down the concourse, ate at a restaurant, shopped for friends, and watched some television. You even sat at the window and watched the planes land and take off. You observed people getting on and off planes, overheard conversations about the trips people took, and thought about the remarkable fact that those huge contraptions can defy gravity and circle the globe. Then after two hours of experiencing the concourse, you headed home.

Why would anyone do this? The concourse is important and crucial to the flying experience, but the purpose of an airport does not revolve around the concourse. The concourse is designed to get people on and off planes. We go to airports because of the airplanes, not the concourse.

We could compare the act of walking up and down the concourse without ever getting on a plane to groups that settle for Personal Improvement and Lifestyle Adjustment. Just as some of the new airports have top-rate restaurants, stores you might find at a mall, and comfortable seating, we can work very hard to make these groups more attractive, more user-friendly, and easier to lead. But by doing so, each bell and whistle we add to normal small groups that make it easier to *huddle and cuddle* covers up the reality that there are missional planes waiting to be boarded by God's people. Getting people to return to our meetings is a good thing, but if that is the end of group life then we are missing the larger picture.

I first realized that meeting attendance is not the ultimate goal of group life one night when half my group did not show up to the meeting. At first I was tempted to be discouraged because I grew up in a church where the primary measurement of church life was how large the attendance report was in the weekly bulletin. But then it hit me: I knew where each person was that night, and various members of the group had spent time together outside the meeting. In addition, a few from the group had interacted with some friends who lived close by and had ministered to them.

When the focus of group life is primarily focused on the meeting, we limit the gospel, the Good News of Jesus, to what can happen through an official meeting. When groups first start out, this is exciting and challenging because it is new and the group is learning how to share Jesus's Good News with others. Over time, however, the experience of the Good News wanes. Groups go through relational ups and downs and the excitement passes. Group meetings often become another weekly commitment instead of an experience where a group is seeing and sharing how the Good News is moving in their lives. Over time, groups in this limited gospel experience usually take one of four paths:

1. They continue on in perpetuity in this fair-to-middlin' normal experience. They aren't radical, but the group still has enough value to people that they want to continue.
2. The entire group breaks up or individual members decide to do something different, often finding a different group, a new

study series they prefer, or a different time that fits their schedule better.

3. A few members of the group catch a vision for something more than the normal group experience and then join with some people from other groups who have a similar vision. Then they begin to test out ways to be a missional small group.

4. The group as a whole catches a vision for more, and they enter into a time of Relational Revision where they can learn together what it means to be a missional small group.

Being Prepared to Relearn the Gospel

If you bought a plane ticket, drove to the airport, and only saw rows of planes and no concourse, it would be quite confusing. How would you determine the right plane for you? How would your luggage be sorted? Where would you wait to board?

Many Christians in North America have a similar experience when they look at the radical call to missional community. They are attracted to the idea of being on mission, they want to do it in community, and they know the normal groups are not enough. At the same time, they don't entirely know what it means to board a plane that will take them into mission. As a result, groups often continue as they have been and simply add some kind of service project or evangelism outing on top of their normal group experience. While their intentions are good, most groups still walk among the airplanes wondering how to get on.

We cannot ignore our context if we are going to be good missionaries in our own land. We must be realistic about the lifestyle of most of the people in North America and recognize that adding a service or outreach project on top of our already overwhelmed lives will not change much of anything. We need to have the space in our lives together to talk about what the gospel looks, feels, and sounds like at this time in history.

I lead a team that works with lots of groups comprised of good people who love God with all they have. But their lives are full of trying to keep up with work, raise kids, and deal with an economy that is less than favorable. The leaders of these groups want to do something radical in their group life together, but we have to deal with reality, not pipe dreams. We cannot throw out a vision for missional community and simply expect people to start living radical lives. These people need places to process what the gospel looks like so they can come to an *ah-ha* moment and see how Personal Improvement and Lifestyle Adjustment are not enough. While such groups are not the end goal, they play an essential role in the church at this time in history.[1]

I wonder if Moses had similar thoughts when he led the Israelites out of Egypt. God sent him to Egypt and empowered him to perform ten miracles. Then he led the Israelites on a trek across the desert expecting to take them into the Promised Land. Look at the map in Figure 3 on the next page. Draw a line from Egypt to Canaan, which is the area promised to Israel.

If Moses had led the people on that direct path, it would have been about a three-week journey. But notice the journey the Israelites took. They went south and then wandered in the wilderness for forty years. Following the cloud and the pillar of fire meant they had to trust God for what he was doing to shape them to be God's people. They needed the wilderness experience as a time of preparation for a larger vision. But the wilderness was not the end game. God promised them a land, and the ultimate vision was for them to enter that land and be God's people there.

The journey toward the vision of missional community is very similar. It starts with the confession that our current small group experiences are not the ultimate goal. The stories of Improvement and Adjustment, while good—they are much better than being back in Egypt—are not the Promised Land. There is a Jordan River that divides Improvement and Adjustment from Revision and Re-creation.

The experiences of the Relational Revision and Missional Re-creation are remarkably different from Improvement and Adjustment groups. But that does not make Improvement and Adjustment unimportant. If we are going to actually move people into God's mission, we need group experiences that meet them where they are. In other words, if the goal is to get on the plane, we need a concourse that will help people do so.

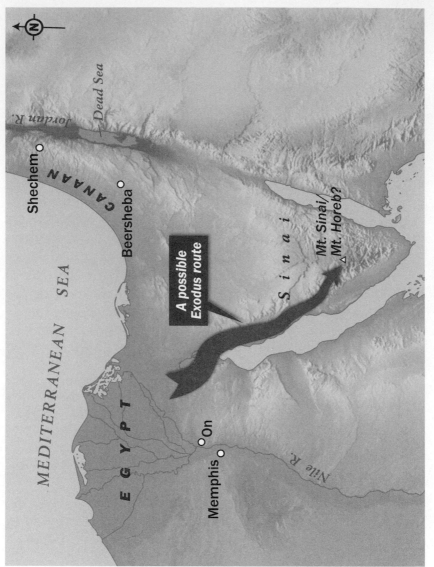

Figure 3

How Improvement and Adjustment Groups Prepare

The wilderness experience was not God's end goal for the people of Israel; he knew he had to prepare them for the Promised Land experience. In the same way, Improvement and Adjustment experiences of group life can be used to prepare people for God's mission in this world. But we must be clear up front or people will become satisfied with walking around in the wilderness. The wilderness wandering experience is meant to lead us to the Jordan River, where we have to make a choice to do life a different way and submit ourselves to an alternative pattern of life.

You may find yourself leading or participating in a normal small group right now or in the near future. If you want to shift your group from being a normal group that has settled for the normal of the wilderness to a group that is being prepared to cross the Jordan River, then there are a few practical things you can do:

1. Avoid judging or criticizing the normal group experience. Most people have to see a new vision in place in their local church before they can understand it. And for many, the normal small group experience has been a great blessing, especially when compared to what they had before joining a group. Instead of criticizing the normal experience, begin to talk about how the group can become something different. Listen to one another in the group and see what God is saying through others. Ask questions about how the group can be different and allow the group to contribute to a new way of life together. While it might not be that radical now, it could lead to something in the future that is.

2. Recognize that leading groups through the preparation phase of the wilderness will be programmatic in nature. And there is plenty of good training, curriculum, and information to help leaders form effective groups that will move people through Improvement and Adjustment. Of course, the danger is that people become satisfied with these experiences because they are better than anything they have had thus far. I think of all the fruit that has come out of the forty-day small group campaigns that have been made popular by Saddleback Church

and Rick Warren's book *The Purpose Driven Life*. And now there are resources like *Activate*, by Nelson Searcy, and *The Sticky Church*, by Larry Osborne, that equip people to do programmatic groups in a semester timeframe. And some of these short-term groups will actually live in ways that tell the missional story of revision and re-creation, but most will not. If you find your group members catching a vision for something different and wanting to be more than a group that simply meets on a regular basis, then capture that moment. Talk with a pastor or a church leader and attain some tools that will help your group process what it means to be on mission.

3. Be realistic. At this point in history, most small groups in North American churches are going to tell the stories of Improvement and Adjustment. That is just reality. And to get together once a week or twice a month and go through a Bible study is important and very helpful, even if the leader is simply a host who does not have to do much more than push *play* on the DVD player. If you find yourself ready to experiment with more and your group does not express such an interest, see if you can find four or five others who share your passion and then begin to practice the missional rhythms that are expressed in the second part of this book.

4. Get equipped to deal with conflict. It seems that God uses conflict within a group as much as anything else to prepare people for a missional future. And it also seems that Satan uses conflict as much as anything else to halt a missional future. Almost every small group leader training course has a session on the fact that conflict will happen, but it is not enough for the leader to know about the reality of relational turmoil. The entire group needs to learn some basic skills in relating and listening to one another through conflict. A couple of good resources that can help groups develop these skills are *Caring Enough to Confront*, by David Augsburger, and *Relationships: A Mess Worth Making*, by Tim Lane and Paul Tripp.

5. Process the future of your group with a coach or a pastor. Often normal groups express little need for input from another leader. But when conversations about being a group that moves

beyond normal into missional begin, the input from a leader outside the group can be especially important.

6. Refuse to simply add some kind of service project or outreach initiative to your group experience and call that missional. As an alternative, take a more relational route. Build relationships with some people who are underresourced and listen to their stories and their needs. Or befriend some people in your neighborhood without any secret motivation to get them to pray a prayer or to come to your group. Simply listen to them, share life, and see what God is already doing in their lives.

Crossing the Jordan River

The journey across the Jordan River cannot be forced. Leaders cannot make people do missional small groups. In fact, we cannot even run them through a set of classes, have them read a book, and give them some outreach homework to get them across the river. The journey is not one of top-down enforcement in which the top leadership can stand before people and declare the vision for missional life and then expect them to jump on board. While most will affirm the vision, they won't be able to comprehend the radical nature of crossing the Jordan and commit to it if it is forced on them from the top.

A small group in Iowa caught a vision for being more than a nice group that met each week to study the Bible and support one another. Over time they built a relationship with a family who had lived in poverty for generations. Instead of doing the normal group thing and ministering to the family as an act of kindness, they decided to invite this family to be part of the group. They shared with them that being part of this group was not about attending a meeting but about sharing life. And because of their difficult life situation, the established group members took it upon themselves to disciple this family into healthy life patterns. Of course, this meant traditional spiritual discipleship, but for them it also meant getting into their lives, their habits, and the way they handled money.

We cannot simply plan to make things like this happen. God is calling his people to defy the gravitational pull of our FedEx culture and allow the Spirit to generate something totally new and different.

We learn it or in some ways catch it as we are shaped for mission. We need to be prepared for mission, not just plan it and do it. This is hard to understand for modern, Western, make-it-happen types. We are trained in the world to lead, to cast vision, and to get people excited about that vision so that they will do something about it. So why doesn't this apply when it comes to being missional?

To play a different set of life rhythms is not something we learn to do from the pastor's new vision or because we have a new structure called *missional small groups*. Instead it is something we learn to do through experiments that add up one after the other to the point that they get deep within us. Then when these experiments take hold, new patterns arise and new norms become predominant. These experiments are not developed by the group leader alone or by a person from outside the group. Instead they are developed by people who begin to talk about how God might move through them in missional ways and then begin to risk new experiments of missional life. A process for experimenting with missional group life is introduced in appendix A.

Moving from normal group life into missional group experiences requires individuals to cross the Jordan and commit to these experiments. While they cross it with others, each individual has to weigh the cost and make a choice to join the journey. For those who feel they are ready to move beyond the normal group experience, here are a few things to consider and pray about:

1. Missional group life invites us to die to ourselves and group life that is based on convenience and self-preservation. When we begin to enter God's mission in this world, it will be messy because relationships and ministry are messy.
2. We must count the cost to enter into missional group life. If you are one of those people who works sixty hours per week or has three kids in nine different extracurricular activities, you will find it hard to add missional living on top of your busy life. You will need to consider how you live, lay it all before God, and allow the Spirit to reshape how you live, not just how you do church.
3. We must repent of the idols of our culture. For instance, North American culture has been shaped by the idol of material-

ism. A recent Best Buy ad campaign was "You, Happier." Our culture has taught us that we will be happier if we have more toys, and while I admit that I would like a new MacBook and a flat-screen television, I need to submit myself to God and recognize how I have bought into the idol of materialism.

4. Ask for the faith of Joshua and Caleb. In the stories of the wilderness wanderings, Moses sent twelve spies into the Promised Land to bring back a report regarding what it would take to possess the land. Ten came back with a negative report, while Joshua and Caleb came back with faith that God could lead them to victory. Forty years later when the people of Israel finally crossed the Jordan River, Joshua and Caleb were the only two still alive who had been slaves in Egypt.

5. Realize that not everyone will cross at the same pace. Some people are risk takers by nature and like to experiment. This does not make those who cross over first more spiritual or give them more value in the church. It simply recognizes that God works through trailblazers in a way that is different from those who maintain and manage. While presenting these ideas at the Willow Creek Group Life Conference, a pastor from Ireland shared about one group of people who all lived within a block of each other. They had come together around a vision to minister to those who lived in one apartment building. They frequently shared meals with one another and shared the gospel with people who would never have come to their church as it operated at that time. They were doing a lot of the practices that are described in part 2 of this book. The pastor was at the point of encouraging them to branch off and start their own church because they were not like the *normal* groups in the church. But after learning the four-stories perspective at the conference, he was able to recognize how he could lead this group of innovators who were experimenting with radical Missional Engagement and how the rest of the church could learn from them.

The gospel, Good News, for those of us in Egypt is that God is leading us out of slavery on a journey to his Promised Land experience. For those in the wilderness, the Good News is that God does not throw us into a radical vision for which he does not prepare us. Instead he is shaping his people for occupation of the Promised Land. The Good News for those who are ready to cross the Jordan is that the Spirit of God dwells within us and empowers us to go where we have not yet been. Ultimately, groups will learn to experience the Good News in fresh ways and have the ability to meet people in their neighborhoods with it. Instead of the Good News being about getting people to come to church meetings to hear a standard message about the gospel, it becomes alive and dynamic as it is embodied by a community within a wider community.

Imagine with me that over the next five years 10 to 20 percent of the people in small groups in North American churches catch a hunger for group life beyond the normal experience. Imagine that they begin to experiment with the practices that play the music of missional group life. Imagine how the Good News of Jesus might transform neighborhoods and the lives of those who are outcasts and marginalized in our culture. If only we can begin with a few and let that trickle down to others. Are you one of those?

Part 2

PRACTICING

5

Three Basic Missional Rhythms

A few years ago Jake, a cell phone programmer from my group, enthusiastically told me about the promotion he had been offered—one that happened to require relocating to another state. He viewed the promotion as a blessing from God, and he wanted me to pray for the transition of his family. Before we prayed I asked him a few questions: "What if where you are today is the best thing for you? This is the first place where your wife has felt a sense of family and support. Your kids have friends, and God is using you here. What if a move is actually a distraction because it will take you a few years to get established there, develop friends, and find what God is calling you to do there?" We talked about the possibility of his finding a new community and participating in mission there, but he needed to think through the impact that following the pattern of the American dream might have upon him and his family.

When individuals count the cost of crossing the Jordan River, they commit to the practices found in the story of Relational Revision. They are invited to sit at the feet of Jesus and learn the musical rhythms that line up with what it means to be the people of God. As I mentioned earlier, Jesus stated in the Sermon on the Mount: "You are the salt of the earth. . . . You are the light of the world. . . . [You are] a city on a hill." God has put his Spirit within his people to be salt, light, and a city not for the sake of themselves but for the sake of God's creation. This has always been God's way of moving in the earth. In Isaiah 60:1–3 he proclaims about the people of Israel:

> Arise, shine, for your light has come, and the glory of the LORD rises upon you. See, darkness covers the earth and thick darkness is over the peoples, but the LORD rises upon you and his glory appears over you. Nations will come to your light, and kings to the brightness of your dawn.

The people of God are called to receive the light of God and display that light in the midst of darkness. Light like this stands out as distinctive because it does not line up with the patterns of darkness of the broader culture. The light metaphor is simply another way of demonstrating that God calls his people to play a contrasting set of musical rhythms from those of the broader culture. These are contrasting rhythms that are part of a contrast society that is called to live out God's dream for creation.

In the story of Relational Revision, we practice the rhythms of the contrast society and learn to live according to God's beautiful dream as we play the new music. My friend Jake realized that he wanted to participate in a way of life that was different than following the American pattern where people move every five years and therefore don't have enough time to establish community. It cost him his job for about two months until the company rehired him in another division. It required him to put his faith in God in a new way and trust that he could learn to play a new song that went against the norm.

Rhythms of Missional Life

When we enter into the story of Relational Revision, we must begin simply, not trying to save the world by biting off more than we can handle. If you want to learn to play a guitar, the music teacher will get you started with three basic chords and some simple strumming. You don't start by trying to mimic Santana without learning the basics. To get started on the journey toward missional small group life, a group should begin with three basic rhythms:

- Missional Communion—the Practices of the Presence
- Missional Relating—the Practices of Agape
- Missional Engagement—the Practices of Engaging the Neighborhood

Being missional is about *who* we are, not just what we do. Therefore, missional life is not simply about the body of Christ having hands and feet so we do something for the world. Living missionally depends on how we relate to God and how we relate to one another as much as on how we relate to those outside the church.

We can easily miss this point. Typically we divide up various aspects of church life into categories of what is done for insiders and what we do for outsiders. Therefore, insiders experience God's presence. Insiders practice love for one another. Then the insiders go and share a message or perform a service project for outsiders. *Missional* then is construed as what is done for outsiders.

Most of the stuff on websites regarding missional life takes up this line of thinking. For instance, it is quite popular to describe these three rhythms as Communion, Community, and Mission. But the problem is that this communicates that mission is something we do on top of the other two areas. It makes being missional a task and removes it from who we are as a people. I know that putting the word *missional* into each of these rhythms might feel awkward because that is not how we think about being missional, but that is exactly why I construe it this way. We need to think differently in order to get the point.

The way we pray, the way we experience God, the way we interact with each other, and the way we deal with conflict is just as much missional as anything we might do for those outside the church. Let me illustrate: Imagine yourself as a citizen of first-century Ephesus—a city that is only about three miles long and two miles wide. Houses are built right next to one another, and streets are very narrow. A man named Paul and his companions arrive, and they visit the synagogue. Paul teaches and people witness miracles. Then a riot flares up because an idol maker is losing business due to people turning to Jesus (see Acts 19). It is impossible for you to be ignorant of what is going on with Paul and his band. While they do specific actions, such as public healings, with the clear intention of proclaiming their message to *outsiders*, you also observe how they treat each other—the *insiders*. Their singing and Paul's teaching can be heard by passers-by, and the way they relate to one another is visible to all who take an interest. The size of the city and the architecture allows anyone to see inside their lives. This tears down any conception that certain things are for *insider*s and others are for *outsiders*.

Now I know that we don't live in first-century Ephesus. Our architecture and the size of our cities create a completely different atmosphere because modern homes and neighborhoods are quite private compared to ancient homes. Herein lies the challenge and the reason experimentation is required. In order for a group to do its life together before God's presence in a way that others can see, it must be worked out in a way that fits the specific location and culture of a neighborhood. This is what missionaries do when they enter a foreign country. They don't enter with a predetermined plan for how they will do church. They listen to how they can show Jesus to the people of that country in ways that are appropriate to the culture.

The following chapters present these three basic rhythms along with specific practices that a group can adopt so that the group can get started playing the music that makes a difference in the world. Before diving into the specific rhythms and practices, there are five things to know that will help you start the music:

1. Many of these basic practices are spiritual disciplines that have become commonplace in books by such authors as Dallas Willard, John Ortberg, Eugene Peterson, Richard Foster, and others.[1] At first it might not be obvious how some of these practices relate to small group life. As I observe the way normal people apply the spiritual disciplines in their lives, I see that most people apply them individualistically. Community is often one of the disciplines alongside others. I would like to invite us to think differently: community is actually the context in which we do the disciplines. Spiritual formation is not something I do alone and then contribute to the community.

2. There are twenty-one different practices that I discuss in the following chapters—seven for each of the three rhythms. Because a group is on a learning path together, there is no way

a group can begin with all of them at once. I suggest a group look over the twenty-one and pick three—one from each of the three chapters. Appendix A provides a thirteen-step process for determining how a group can get started with these three practices.

3. I have written the twenty-one practices in a devotional, reflective style with only a few practical suggestions about how to implement that practice. My reasoning for this is twofold: First, there are many practical resources available that can supplement this book and give you practical steps beyond what I provide. I have listed some of the best resources in appendix B. Second, I want to invite you and others in your group to reflect and listen to God together about the specific practices you will implement before you start doing something. By nature I am a type-A, get-it-done, make-something-happen person. But through the years I have found that if we want to see things in a different light, we must first of all slow down and reflect, talk with one another, and listen to God and others about what needs to change. We are not simply talking about surface-level change that can be done by adopting a few how-to tactics. We are talking about changing how we do life and begin to play new music. This only happens as people talk about that which lies beneath the surface. For instance, middle-class suburbanites might see how God has called them to relate to and befriend the underresourced. To actually do this, it will require them to talk about how they spend their time and how they will have to change in order to make time for this calling. It will also require them to process how they have judged the underresourced and how they have jumped to conclusions about them that have caused them to ignore those people in the past.

4. The specific ways these practices are played will depend upon specific neighborhoods and the needs of the communities in which the group is set. It will also depend upon the specific tradition from which the people come. For instance, the way a group from a Lutheran church practices these rhythms will be very different than the way a group from a Baptist church does. This is one reason why the input from a pastor, coach, or church leader from outside the group is so crucial. As stated

in the introduction, this book only serves as an introductory music book. It works best with a music teacher as a guide. If you don't have one, try to connect with another group that is on a similar journey and learn from one another.

5. To help facilitate conversations around these practices, there is space at the end of each practice for you to write some notes, reflections, and comments. Read slowly and listen to the Spirit as you do. Write down what you sense. Ask yourself these three questions as you read the reflections:

- What is God saying to me as I read?
- What does this mean for my life?
- What impact does this have on the way we do small group?

What's the Point?

Missional Communion, Missional Relating, and Missional Engagement are not ends in and of themselves. They are ways that we practice being God's people in the midst of a world that treats people nonrelationally. The ways of our world set patterns in which people are objectified and treated like machines. The nature of *agape* love is to value people no matter what their practical value. The three rhythms of missional life put feet on what it means to be the bride of Christ and demonstrate God's missional life in our world.

Missional Communion, Missional Relating, and Missional Engagement are my way of labeling the spiritual disciplines as seen through the lens of communal as opposed to individual practice. Discovering the spiritual disciplines as communal practices has been refreshing for me. I no longer have to be the ultraserious spiritual diehard. I don't have to prove to myself and others that I can be radical and committed. It is not about me and what I choose to do as an individual. It is about what we do together that changes me the most.

In the first century the Jewish people had been dispersed throughout the Middle East after the Babylonian exile. This was known as the Diaspora. God's people had been dispersed rather than centralized. In a similar way the New Testament people of God were dispersed from Jerusalem with the persecution. (See the first few chapters of Acts.) The Christian movement of the first century was a decentralized movement—one that was not organized from a Jerusalem center but took on creative manifestations throughout the Roman Empire. In similar ways, this is the call upon small groups that are scattered in neighborhoods, apartment buildings, office buildings, college campuses, and elsewhere. Missional small groups provide a context of being God's dispersed people together, where they have the opportunity to parade the reality of the kingdom of God in front of a watching public.

6

The Rhythm of Missional Communion with God

I grew up in a church that belonged to a denomination that has probably emphasized evangelism more than any other. In every evangelism seminar or class I attended, the presentations focused on ways to talk to unbelievers about Jesus. To be honest, I always had the impression that evangelism meant talking people into something that they did not want. It just felt a bit inauthentic.

Until our group met Linda, I had never realized that how the church prays can actually be one of the most genuine and authentic ways of sharing our faith with those who don't know Jesus. Linda was a single woman who lived next door to us. We met her at a pool party and then invited Linda and her brother to our home for a meal. Our intentions were simply to be her friend, not necessarily to get her to come to our group or get her saved. But because our group met in our home and we freely shared with her what transpired in our groups, she was well aware of what we did and even observed how we related to God.

Then Linda was diagnosed with breast cancer. We did not have to go to her and force prayer upon her. She came to us and timidly asked if we would pray. No quick miracle resulted from our prayers, but lots of little miracles did. During her time of going through chemo, we stood with her and prayed for her, and yes, she started attending our group and then later committed her life to Jesus.

Relating to God is basic and foundational to anything we do missionally, but for some reason, we don't often talk about this. When I read most books on small groups, little is said in them about God's presence. They contain a lot of tactical information and practical skill training. I read articles on group leadership and it is easy to find information on how to ask good questions, ideas for creative study materials, and instructions on what leaders do in order to be effective. I would rather be part of a group that gets all of the tactical stuff wrong but yet encounters Jesus on a regular basis than miss out on the presence of God while getting the technical steps to group leadership right.

Jesus says, "Where two or three come together in my name, there am I with them" (Matt. 18:20). As I read the various stories about God's people in the Scriptures, the presence of God is a significant marker of who belongs to him. The cloud leads the people of Israel by day and the pillar of fire by night. The presence of God fills the temple on the day Solomon dedicates it. In the New Testament, we are told that the coming of the kingdom of God will be marked by a return of God's presence in Jerusalem. We don't have to work very hard to conclude that God's people are made distinct from the broader culture by God's presence.

In what follows you will find seven practices that help groups move into Missional Communion with God.

Practice: Worship

Ascribe to the LORD the glory due his name; worship the LORD in the splendor of his holiness.

Psalm 29:2

I hate wasting time. I like to get things done, and I love to get a lot of things done quickly. There are few things more painful to me than a long line when I don't have a book, a traffic jam when my cell phone battery is dead, or a boring meeting when I cannot answer emails. Wasting time is a royal pain.

Recently I have been thinking about my view of wasting time and how it actually works against something that God values greatly: worship. Marva Dawn refers to worship as a "royal waste of time" in her book by that title. She writes, "To worship the Lord is—in the world's eyes—a waste of time. . . . By engaging in it, we don't accomplish anything useful in our society's terms."[1] And since most group leaders want to create groups that members deem valuable, it can be tempting to move beyond worship and use the time for activities that people think are useful or practical. Always doing what comes easily in a group, however, can actually work against doing groups in a way that causes us to stand out from the world.

But Small Group Singing Is Awkward

For some groups, worship comes naturally. When someone in your group knows a few worship songs and can lead with a guitar, then all seems well. But what about the rest of us who do not play the guitar and don't sit around singing worship songs in our spare time? What about the groups that are full of people who are tone deaf or who just like to "get into the meat" and talk about the Bible? What about groups that just want to get together to connect or play a sport? Or what about groups that are focused on social activism and don't have time to focus on worship?

In our modern church experience, worship has been equated to singing. As a result, groups that are inclined to this expression of worship will find little challenging in this practice thus far. But small group worship does not mean small group singing. I have had many small group singing experiences where we sang all of the *right* worship songs, but we did not worship. Instead we were following the popular worship song pattern, and everyone liked it.

On the other hand, some from the "we don't have to sing" camp argue that our "spiritual act of worship" is to "offer [our] bodies as living sacrifices" (Rom. 12:1 NIV). In other words, we don't need a designated time for worship since the Bible tells us that worship is really about total life surrender, not about having a specific time for worship. But this is like saying, "Well, since we just talked *about* God for the last thirty minutes and he is here with us all the time and heard what we were saying about him, we don't actually need to spend time talking *to* him." I don't do that with my friends; why would I do it with God?

The point is not what we do when we worship but who we encounter. Marva Dawn's words point us in the right direction:

> Worship is a royal waste of time, but indeed it is royal, for it immerses us in the regal splendor of the King of the cosmos. The churches' worship provides opportunities for us to enjoy God's presence in corporate ways that take us out of time and into the eternal purposes of God's kingdom. As a result, we shall be changed—but not because of anything we do. God, on whom we are centered and to whom we submit, will transform us by his Revelation of himself.[2]

All of this seems a bit mysterious and uncontrollable. There are no controllable outcomes with worship, just as there are none in how a conversation will go with a friend. Sometimes there is a profound connection, and other times it feels rather humdrum. But worship is about providing an opportunity to connect with the eternal Father, Son, and Spirit, to relate to the God who is radically different than us. We cannot control this relationship, and therefore we cannot control the mystery of connecting with God in worship.

When we worship, we are simply developing one of the habits of those who call themselves Christians. The world has its habits and the church its own. The act of developing habits requires steady repetition. Worship is not something we "get down" and then move on to something else. Whether profound or humdrum, it is one of the things that shapes our lives as God's people, and of course it might feel awkward if we view it through the need to be useful.

Practice Lessons

You can create the best small group worship experience imaginable. You might have a worship team member lead it or even use a cutting-edge interactive DVD. The people might even sing out loud and show great emotion. But we can still miss God. Some of the best times of worship have had none of these things in place. In fact, one of the best ways to invite people to encounter God is to break out of the rut and enter into God's presence in an unexpected way.

In his book *A Pocket Guide to Leading a Small Group*, Dave Earley identifies fourteen different forms of worship in the Scriptures:

1. Being silent in awe (Isaiah 6)
2. Kneeling or lying face down in absolute surrender (Revelation 4)
3. Confessing sin (2 Samuel 12; Psalm 51)
4. Shouting in thanksgiving (Pss. 42:4; 66:1–2; 71:23; 98:4; 100:1)
5. Trembling in reverence (Rev. 5:8)
6. Resolving to obey (Genesis 22)
7. Praising in the midst of difficulties (Job 1)
8. Giving God offerings out of gratitude (2 Samuel 24; 1 Kings 8; 2 Chronicles 5–6)
9. Yielding your will (Jonah 2)
10. Dancing (2 Samuel 6; Ps. 149:3)
11. Singing for joy (Exodus 15; Pss. 21:13; 63:45; 71:22)
12. Playing musical instruments (Pss. 43:4; 71:22; 98:4–6)
13. Clapping your hands (Ps. 47:1)
14. Lifting your hands (Pss. 63:4; 134:2)[3]

Small group worship can take on many different forms, singing being only one. Many use recorded songs on CDs when there is no one in the group who can play an instrument. Other options include listening quietly to a song in reflection, reading a psalm aloud and responding, reading a responsive reading such as Psalm 136, each person sharing one thing God has done for them over the last week, offering short prayers of thanksgiving for who God is, and reading a liturgy. Some might use a prayer book like the *Book of Common Prayer*. A group could take a ten-minute walk around the neighborhood with the challenge to see what God is doing there and give expression to that.

All of these forms of worship have the intent of getting people to turn to God and away from self. Most of us come together in our groups fully aware of the stress and problems we face. Groups become a place to dump this on others who have just as many things they need to dump. Without worship, people turn in on themselves and share life together based on good advice and their best logic.

Worship calls us out of the normal to see things from a different perspective.

Following Jesus

The writer of Hebrews tells us, "Therefore, since we have a great high priest who has ascended into heaven, Jesus the Son of God, let us hold firmly to the faith we profess. . . . Let us then approach God's throne of grace with confidence, so that we may receive mercy and find grace to help us in our time of need" (4:14, 16). The role of the high priest is to be the lead worshiper of the people of God. Jesus's life on earth was characterized by worship, and he is now worshiping in heaven on our behalf.

Some might take this and use guilt to motivate the act of worship, saying, "Since we are supposed to be like Jesus, we must also worship." The emphasis here is on us and our actions of worship. If there is anything that will undermine worship in a small group, it is the forced expectation of worship. When this is the case, it can become spiritual performance for the sake of acceptance by the other group members.

But if Jesus is our great High Priest, the great eternal worship leader, then our response of worship is simply our participation in his worship. We worship *in Christ*. This is like playing basketball with Michael Jordan. It does not matter how good you are at basketball; your team is automatically good because he is part of it. He is the greatest of all time, and you get to go along for the ride. Our small group worship might be awkward, rough, and unpolished. We might even be embarrassed by it. But our worship experience is not the point. Joining Jesus in what he does continually is what matters. And thereby, we are transformed into his likeness. What a mystery; what a privilege!

Use the following space to record your reflections on this practice:

Practice: Practicing the Presence

Now about the gifts of the Spirit, brothers and sisters, I do not want you to be uninformed. . . . There are different kinds of gifts, but the same Spirit distributes them. There are different kinds of service, but the same Lord. There are different kinds of working, but in all of them and in everyone it is the same God at work.

1 Corinthians 12:1, 4–6

When the conversation related to the Holy Spirit and the gifts of the Spirit, the apostle Paul never seemed to lack for words. He wanted people to be informed about how God worked in and through his people. Today, many seem to be quite focused on God's power and the gifts, while at the same time there are many others who avoid it at all cost. Either way, we miss the point. Paul's first focus lay not on the gifts and power as much as on the presence of God in the midst of his people. Paul could talk freely about spiritual gifts because the house groups he led regularly encountered God's presence.

When we talk about small groups and God's presence, the place to begin is with these questions: Have we learned to do small groups as if God is not present with us? Is it possible that our carefully designed curriculum on which we spend lots of money can actually distract us from the fact that the Spirit of God lives in us and wants to manifest through us?

Not about Being Charismatic

Asking these questions is crucial no matter your tradition or church background—even charismatic or Pentecostal. All churches develop traditions, forms for doing church life, which create a set pattern of how their gatherings work. Traditions are not necessarily evil because we need them to help shape and define us as a people. Every church

75

tradition, however, can become simply a habit that we do without encountering the reality of God's presence.

God invites us into a relationship, but sadly, we often fall into a rut and simply do our meeting according to our tradition. For some the rut is Bible study, for others it is following a particular liturgy, and for others it is an emotional experience or a specific way of doing spiritual gifts. In many cases we have grown so accustomed to the way we do our life as God's people that if God did show up in our groups, we would not entirely know what was happening and would simply go back to the way we have always done things.

Recently I read a stack of books on small groups that have been released over the last two or three years. It saddens me how little most of these books have to say about God. They address key sociological principles about how to lead small groups. They explain how to set up small group structures and get people connected in community. They even teach people how to lead Bible discussions. But regarding how the Spirit of God might work through a small group of people, it looks to me like we are *uninformed* or at least *under-informed*.

There is a lot of talk about how to do small groups and little actual talk about the God who desires to show up at those small groups. How can we talk about spiritual gifts if our small group imagination is primarily shaped by sociological principles, small group structures, and Bible study questions? Through the Internet and published resources, we have more small group tools at our disposal today than during any other era in church history. I hope these resources are helpful. But if our imagination about small group life is primarily shaped by questions about sociological principles, small group structures, and small group study materials, then I wonder if we are asking the right questions.

Relating to God

Sometimes I reflect on the New Testament and imagine what Paul might say to the church today. I wonder if he might say something like, "If you want to be used of God in spiritual gifts, then start with the expectation that you will encounter God's presence together. The gifts are gifts of God's Spirit. They are not yours for using as you will." Of course, our question in response to Paul would be, "How do you do this?" Then in my imagination I hear him responding, "What exactly do you mean? How else would you relate to God? . . . You relate."

Even as I imagine this, I get frustrated with the vagueness in my own imagination. I want a how-to manual for encountering God's presence in a group. But that is not how relationships work. We cannot apply a formula to relationships. As soon as we make a relationship about principles or steps, we have turned the relationship into something that is not an encounter with the other person. God cannot be objectified this way. Relationships are about taking the risk of the give-and-take and the discovery of the other person as we make mistakes along the way.

Practice Lessons

We learn to relate on the road of relating, not in a classroom or from an insightful book on relationships. And the same is true in our relationship with God. We just have to start relating to him together in our groups. We simply need to realize that we have to learn together how we are going to encounter the presence of God together. This is not something we just do as individuals and then talk about at our group meetings. We must learn to create the space where we can encounter God as a group. For most this will require a few changes in the way we typically do groups:

1. Change the expectations. If people expect to gather around a Bible study or a DVD curriculum or even around social interaction, the presence of the Spirit will be minimal. When doing normal small groups that live out the stories of Improvement and Adjustment, the focus may very well be on the content being discussed. But when we move into the story of Relational Revision, we are learning to be a group that encounters God's presence. The group must understand this subtle shift. You may still use the same curriculum, but the purpose lies not on learning something so that you can be more informed but on listening to what God is saying as the Spirit moves through the group.
2. Shorten the Bible study to make room to wait on God together. In most small group curriculum, there are simply too many

questions listed. And if you ask them all, the group will remain primarily a thinking group. Instead of spending the forty minutes on Bible discussion, you could shorten it to twenty minutes and then provide a time of silence or listen to some instrumental music. Ask people to listen to God and afterward share what they heard.

3. Vary the agenda from week to week. You don't have to change everything, but adding some twists to the time together helps people realize that it is about relationships, not about meetings. Start the meeting with a short walk around the neighborhood; ask someone else to lead the Bible discussion; play a board game for half of the meeting—these are just a few ideas that can help people escape the rut.

4. Eat together. You might be surprised by this one, but food is essential to connecting with one another and inviting God's presence into our midst.

When we think about moving beyond normal groups, we need to move beyond the habits of our inherited traditions. We might know how to fill a meeting with answering Bible study questions, singing songs, and even praying for each other's requests. But these things we know how to do can stand in the way of relating to the God who speaks in a *still, small voice*. Unless we hear this voice and make room in our groups to encounter this God, we will miss God's leading and empowering that we need to participate in God's mission.

Use the following space to record your reflections on this practice:

Practice: Alone Together

Then a great and powerful wind tore the mountains apart and shattered the rocks before the LORD, but the LORD was not in the wind. After the wind there was an earthquake, but the LORD was not in the earthquake. After the earthquake came a fire, but the LORD was not in the fire. And after the fire came a gentle whisper. When Elijah heard it, he pulled his cloak over his face and went out and stood at the mouth of the cave.

1 Kings 19:11–13

With every relationship come expectations. Whether in friendship, in marriage, or with colleagues, each party expects certain actions and communication from the other person. It is unavoidable. This is no less true of our relationship with God.

Even the great Old Testament prophet Elijah struggled with expectations regarding his relationship with God. The encounter between Elijah and God recorded above comes after one of the most spectacular events recorded in the Bible. In chapter 18 of 1 Kings we read about a contest between the God of Elijah and the prophets of Baal. Elijah challenges the prophets of Baal to entreat their god to light a sacrifice with fire. After hours of religious performance, their god fails the test. On the other hand, Elijah pours water on the sacrifice three times and says a simple prayer, and fire falls from heaven and consumes the sacrifice and even the altar. This simple story overflows with the magnificent and is full of action, intrigue, and miracles.

But the encounter with God in 1 Kings 19 is quite different. Here the Lord is not in the spectacular, the loud, or the magnificent. Here there are no miracles, no crowds, and no fame. At this point it is just Elijah and the Lord, and the Lord comes in a different way than Elijah expected.

Most Christians know that they should connect with God. We have been taught to have quiet times, read devotionals such as those of Oswald Chambers, and study the Bible. All of these are good practices for individuals, but the practices in and of themselves do not necessarily form the rhythm that produces the missional music of God's people. They can play a part, but sadly, they can actually reinforce the individualism that is a controlling mind-set of our broader culture. We need to practice personal disciplines, but we

79

need to learn how to do them in the midst of a community so that these practices can be done together rather than alone.

In order to understand what it means to be alone together, we need to think through a couple of barriers to such an experience.

Barrier 1: We Are Never Alone

In our current experience of the world, we are never alone. We are surrounded not by the spectacular or the magnificent but by the constant hum of life. Each day overflows with activity, commitments, and appointments. Most of us could work fifteen hours straight and still feel that we are behind. Then add the slew of conversations with others—most of which are surface conversations about what has happened or what will happen because they are related to daily activities. Then put on top of this the noise of life that surrounds us. Even when alone physically, most have the radio, television, iPod, or Internet piping in some level of noise.

In many ways we live in a culture in which people are afraid to truly be alone, because in such an experience, we don't like what we see. We are afraid to be with ourselves, to sit and reflect, to listen to what is going on in our hearts. As a result, we cling to activity, to conversations, to noise, and ultimately to others. Often we cling to people in groups in order to survive life, but this can actually steal life from the community and suck it dry.

Community is cultivated by those who know how to be alone and thereby have something to offer others. Togetherness and aloneness work together as we seek God through both.

Barrier 2: Always Alone

This barrier is not about the experience of loneliness or friendlessness. This is the *always alone* experience that has shaped the imagination of so many Christians when they think about their personal relationship with God. When we think of prayer or having a quiet time or personal devotions, it is related to our individual private relationship with God. Even when there is talk about salvation, it is related to a personal or private vertical relationship with God. It is as though the church is not really necessary because my private beliefs and relationship with God are all that matter.

Over the last few years there has been a resurgence of teaching in the church that emphasizes some of the ancient spiritual practices like "praying the hours," practicing silence and solitude, and *lectio divina*.[4] I love these ancient practices, and they have shaped me for the better. It is easy to adopt the pattern of individualism when implementing these spiritual disciplines. And while doing them alone is helpful, the missional question requires us to ask how we as a community can do them together.

This takes us back to the story of Elijah. After hearing the "gentle whisper," Elijah complained to God that he was totally alone, that there were none left in Israel who were devoted to God. In response God told him of Elisha and seven-thousand others who had not bowed to Baal.

It is a dangerous thing to elevate oneself to a position of *always alone* before God. Dietrich Bonhoeffer writes, "Whoever cannot stand being in community should beware of being alone."[5] When always alone, we make ourselves the judge of others. We become critics of those in the group, and our individual needs and meeting those needs become our central concern.

But there is another perspective.

Practice Lessons

"Only as we stand within the community can we be alone, and only those who are alone can live in the community. Both belong together. Only in the community do we learn to be properly alone; and only in being alone do we learn to live properly in community."[6] These words by Bonhoeffer hit the nail on the head; however, most of us fail to see how this profound statement impacts our life together. We apply it in our normal group life in this way: When we are together, we do stuff together. But when we are apart, my relationship with God is my responsibility and I do what I need to do to cultivate it. Such a perspective misses the point.

When we cross over into missional community, we discover that when we are alone before God we do so together. It is not a *me and God* experience. I don't go to God by myself. I don't go on a private retreat by myself. I don't go on a quite walk with just God and me. Those in my community go with me even when I am alone. I take them with me because they are a part of me. Contrary to what most might think, this does not devalue my *personal* relationship with God. It actually trains me in the ways of relating to God alone as it aligns my expectations with those that actually fit who God is and how he communicates.

I first read of the concept of being *alone together* in the book *The Mystery of Marriage*, in which the authors talk about being alone while sitting in one another's presence. This is a great experience in marriage, but what about being alone together when the individuals in a community are not physically present to one another? How might the community of individuals be alone before God but do it together? The options are numerous and the process is quite simple. Any of the following spiritual disciplines can be done together:

- Choose a good devotional book and read it together.
- Practice *lectio divina* around a common Scripture. For instance, imagine you are studying Romans 12:1–2. The group could commit to reading these verses every day and ask these four questions as they reflect on it:
  1. Read the passage. What stands out to you?
  2. Reflect on the point that stands out to you. What comes to mind as you reflect on this passage?
  3. Pray what you see in this passage. Turn any insight you have into a prayer.
  4. Wait on God. What do you sense God speaking to you?
- Use a book like the *Divine Hours* or the *Book of Common Prayer* as a personal prayer guide.
- Fast together on the same day or over the same few days.

Finally, a basic practice that can shape being alone together is to simply commit to pray for others in the group and listen to God for one another. Imagine how phone conversations, Facebook updates, email interaction, and personal encounters with one another might be transformed if we simply pray for each other before we interact. This might seem quite simple, and in reality it is. If we understand how God sees others in the group, our relationships with them will be transformed.

Use the following space to record your reflections on this practice:

Practice: Listening Together

And God said, . . .

Genesis 1–Revelation 22

God has spoken, and God continues to speak today. The Bible declares "God is love" (1 John 4:8,16), which implies that he is relational and therefore speaks to his people. If we are to live relationally with God and others, we need to hear God *his* way, and this is best done together.

Listening Alone

So many people have been turned off by any talk of listening to God because too many have tried to listen to God in a way that does not fit how God speaks—in isolation. By myself, I can come up with all kinds of things that I might sense God is saying to me. Or in prayer, *I* have an inner impression and *I* interpret that impression and go tell another person, "God told me . . ." This can be especially destructive when I say God has told me something about that other person. I can become the critic of others, judging them and causing harm along the way.

The "God said to me . . ." or "God told me . . ." line is dangerous. It's a line that is used frequently at Bible college in the dating scene. "God told me that you would be my wife," or "God told me to break up with you." But it is also found in other places: "God told me to quit my job and trust him for provision," or "God told me that I am to lead worship in the group."

The examples of listening the wrong way are endless. And sadly, this listening alone and the resulting weirdness make the rhythm of listening to God unattractive. It does not, however, take weird stuff to make this rhythm distasteful. A few boring quiet times during which we only operate out of logic and information can turn an opportunity to hear God into a legalistic act of boredom.

Listening Together

A few years ago I felt God leading me to move my family 1,300 miles from Texas to Minnesota. This came out of long times of being alone with God, but there were many others who were providing input and speaking into our decision as a family. I never came out of those times with God saying, "God told me . . ." Instead, I was saying, "I sense that God might be leading . . ." We hear God best as individuals in the context of humbly submitting what we sense to others in community. The community experience in a small group provides a set of relationships whereby we can listen to and for one another. In such a context I don't have to figure out my life alone. I don't have to make big decisions by myself. I don't even have to figure out if what I am sensing in isolation is of God.

Just meeting weekly in a small group will not necessarily result in the rhythm of listening together. In fact, most of the times I have experienced this listening together has occurred outside of the official meeting time. I might share my concern, my desire, or my sense of what God is saying in the meeting, but the real listening occurs later—when another group member calls me or asks me out for coffee, and then a conversation develops. For such listening to occur, three things have to happen.

1. FOCUS ON JESUS

At the core of anything that God speaks or has spoken is *Jesus*. The historical reality of Jesus taking on human flesh and walking this earth is foundational to all God does and says. Jesus is *the* communication of God. The writer of the book of Hebrews puts it this way:

In the past God spoke to our ancestors through the prophets at many times and in various ways, but in these last days he has spoken to us by his Son, whom he appointed heir of all things, and through whom also he made the universe. The Son is the radiance of God's glory and the exact representation of his being, sustaining all things by his powerful word.

1:1–3

If we want to know what God is like, we need to see what Jesus is like. If we want to hear what God is saying to us today, we need to begin with an encounter with Jesus. We must listen to Jesus because he is the "head of the church" (Eph. 5:23) and the church is the "body of Christ" (1 Cor. 12:27). Therefore, even though Jesus is absent today in body, through the Holy Spirit, he is directly connected to and speaking to the little "bodies of Christ" meeting throughout the world.

Essential to listening to Jesus today is the principle of two or three. He says, "For where two or three come together in my name, there am I with them" (Matt. 18:20). Coming together in the name of Jesus means that the group gathers with a focus on Jesus and who he is. The focus is not so much on Bible study, individuals' needs, or having a good time as it is on the reality that Jesus is with us and in our midst. The way a group focuses on Jesus will vary from week to week because there is no formula to *meeting in Jesus's name*.

There is, however, something very practical that will propel a group forward in relating to Jesus. If all of the pressure to lead a group into the presence of Jesus falls on the shoulders of one leader, this can cause the experience to be awkward or even forced. As a result, the group leader will opt out of the expectation and settle for a *good Bible study* or a nice, fun time. An alternative is for the leader to identify two other people who will work together as a team to lead the meetings. The three enter the group meeting with the clear purpose of *meeting in Jesus's name* after having worked together to come up with a variety of ways to draw people into this reality.[7]

2. Live the Scriptures

God speaks to his church through the Bible. This is how we envision who Jesus is. But there is a problem in most small groups. The

85

kind of listening found in most small groups is primarily shaped by Bible study. We talk about the Scriptures to find out information regarding the meaning of the facts within the Scriptures. Small groups can become a kind of mini theology huddle.

This critique might sound like I am against the study of the Bible. Please don't hear that. I read Bible commentaries just for the fun of it. But there is much more to listening together than just talking about the meaning of a text and sharing opinions about what we think it means.

Listening together to the Scriptures occurs when we hear the grand story of the Bible and begin to participate in it. This can be illustrated by two different approaches to cooking. One is the analytical, precise approach of using recipes that are written out on a card or in a book. The other is illustrated in the way my grandmother used to explain a recipe. When asked how to cook one of her prized meals, she would simply say, "Well, you take some _____ and cover it with _____. Then you combine some _____, a little _____, and a pinch of _____. Combine that with a little water and pour it on top of the _____ and then cook it until it is done." After listening to her explain a few recipes, it became evident that the only way to learn to cook as she did was to be with her in the kitchen. The way she did recipes required *her*, not a piece of paper. Listening to the Scriptures together is not an act of abstraction that can be done by reading type on a page and then lived out. The Scriptures are alive and active, and the way we listen to them is to see them come to life in each other. So we read Scripture together and then together we share its reality in our lives. And in the communities that gather, there should be seasoned followers who know how to live the Scriptures and teach others by living them.

This is much different than a Bible discussion that leads to "life application" where individuals are asked to apply a biblical principle to their individual lives. Instead, it is an experienced reality that organically arises in a group by the Spirit of God as the people in the group share life together around God's Word.

3. Speak the Truth

Eugene Peterson provides a fresh paraphrase of an oft misunderstood verse, 1 Corinthians 14:3. It reads: "But when you proclaim his truth in everyday speech, you're letting others in on the truth so that they can grow and be strong and experience his presence with you" (Message). I love the phrase "proclaim truth in everyday speech," because it calls us out of some kind of superspiritual reality and into the reality that God is present with us in our living, working, laughing, and conversing. Peterson uses these words to translate the word normally rendered *prophesy*. A common translation would read, "But those who prophesy speak to people for their strengthening, encouragement, and comfort." But the word *prophesy* has traditionally been taken out of the ordinary and made to be something only the *spiritual elites* do. In some traditions *prophesy* is something those of the collar do when they preach. In other traditions it is what the especially gifted do when they share an ecstatic "word from the Lord." Common to them both is the idea that to prophesy is to speak during a spiritual service in the church building.

But this is far from Paul's meaning of the word in this context. First of all, they did not have church buildings. We do not know much about when and where they met, but what we can ascertain is that hearing God together was a reality that was woven into their everyday life. God spoke through the churches as they gathered in what we might label a meeting or service but also in the common interaction as communities gathered to share meals, serve each other, and just be with one another.

Truth speaking that was inspired by the Holy Spirit was a shared reality. They were not waiting for official words from the preacher, nor were they waiting for the "thus sayeth the Lord" experience. They simply spoke into one another's lives as they sensed the Spirit of God leading them to do so. Was it perfect? Far from it, as we see in many of Paul's letters. But in this passage we have the simple measurement that any "speaking truth" is truly prophecy of the Spirit if it strengthened, encouraged, or comforted.

Practice Lessons

Here are some ways to begin to practice these things:

1. Focus on Jesus: Identify two or three people in the group who can meet at least once per month outside of the regular meeting

to pray about and participate in leading the group. Talk together about the purpose of the group and work together on how to lead others into the vision of being a missional small group.

2. Live the Scriptures: Identify one or two passages of Scripture that can shape the imagination and life of the group. Scriptures that can prove helpful for this include: Luke 4:18–19; 9:23; Romans 12:1–2; Philippians 2:6–8. Read them together often. Pray them as a group. Reflect together on ways that God is forming you through them.

3. Speak the Truth: As a group, read 1 Corinthians 14:3 and talk about what it means to speak to each other in ways that strengthen, encourage, and comfort. Ask people to think about their words and how they use them in their regular conversations. Then talk about ways you can speak to each other differently so as to encourage one another. Commit to saying at least one encouraging thing to another group member during the coming week; then talk about it when you meet next. This might feel awkward at first, but it can lead to more natural conversation.

Use the following space to record your reflections on this practice:

Practice: Simplicity

Do not store up for yourselves treasures on earth, where moth and rust destroy, and where thieves break in and steal. But store up for yourselves treasures in heaven, where moth and rust do not destroy, and where thieves do not break in and steal.

Matthew 6:19–20

It is okay to talk about spiritual things in the church. We can talk about prayer, living morally upright, "getting saved," God's love for us, and other topics that fit nicely into a sixty- to ninety-minute spiritual escape on Sunday morning. But it is not okay to talk about the spiritual implications related to how we spend our money or our time. Those are private matters that should be left to individual choices.

But the Bible actually speaks quite a lot about these very practical, mundane matters of life. Things like greed, anxiety, self-promotion, and priorities in life fill the pages of God's Word. To limit God to a box labeled "Spiritual" is to miss the point of biblical spirituality. The way we do life in mundane things—like how we handle our money and manage our time—directly impacts our life with God. We often fail to realize how the little decisions we make every day about seemingly insignificant things can actually undermine the rhythms that God has called us to play in this world.

Complex World

It is hard to imagine a world that could be more complex than the one that exists today. But when we look at life a year from now, most likely there will be more issues that bring complexity, not fewer. When computers were being introduced in the early 1970s, government officials predicted that they would change the way we work. They got that right, but they dramatically missed *how* it would change us. They predicted twenty-five- or thirty-hour workweeks because the level of production would increase by so much. LOL (that means "laugh out loud" in text talk). We now can do more with less, but the expectations and demands placed on us increase the more we can do.

Then add the incessant pressure to obtain more stuff. It seems the goal of every manufacturing business is to create more stuff, each with a new element that they must then convince us we cannot live without, even though mankind has been doing quite well without this stuff for a very long time. In 1973 Arthur Gish wrote in his book *Beyond the Rat Race*, "We buy things we do not want to impress people we do not like."[8] If that was true back then, how much more so today?

Richard Foster diagnoses the problem: "We are trapped in a maze of competing attachments. One moment we make decisions on the basis of sound reason and the next moment out of fear of what others will think of us. We have no unity or focus around which our lives are oriented."[9]

Why Be Simple?

Simplicity for the sake of simplicity can turn into legalism and judgment of others who are not simple. Recently a man told me that he has chosen to wear used clothing but that it is not a big deal for him to do so because he really does not care what he wears. But for him to place that expectation on his wife, who cares a great deal how she dresses, is unrealistic. We must be careful when we talk about the use of our time and how we spend money. The excesses eliminated by some might be quite essential to others.

Simplicity is something that results from having what Foster calls a "divine Center."[10] When we "seek first [God's] kingdom and his righteousness" (Matt. 6:33), God begins to reorient our lives so that we have space in our lives to love him and others more. Jesus becomes our vision and focus and then the Spirit of God begins to order our life, our commitments, our priorities, and our spending. If we start by establishing a specific list of acceptable ways to spend our time and money, we only have anxiety about whether we are doing it *right*. And we don't need any more anxiety in this age. But if we understand that simplicity is a way to allow the love of God to move through us more freely, then it becomes a choice of love, not an act of legalism.

Making Room for God

For many, this means that God is the top priority in life, and the way to express this is by inner devotion to God and participation in spiritual activities. In other words, the kingdom is an inner experience that has little to no bearing on my daily life. Others see the kingdom solely as a future reality, and life for Christians here on earth is about survival until Jesus returns. Seeking the kingdom for people with this mind-set is about waiting for the *escape* from this world.

But Jesus says, "The kingdom of God is near" (Luke 21:31). In other words, the kingdom has come up close and personal in the person of Jesus. If the Holy Spirit is the continuing presence of God, then the kingdom remains near. Jesus came to inaugurate a *way of life* while we are on earth, not just a destiny for believers after we die. To seek first the kingdom means that we must make room for the kingdom of God in our lives. If we expect to develop a divine Center without making some hard choices about how we do life, then we are sorely mistaken. Making room in our lives so we can love more freely will require us to make hard choices—choices that go against the flow of our culture.

Practice Lessons

Refer back to page 30 where the overwhelmed FedEx life of Pat was introduced. To shift from this view of doing life that has no center to a divine Center will most likely begin with choosing to eliminate some circles for the sake of making some room for God in our lives.

Take a few minutes and draw out your own Life Rhythms Diagram. Start by putting your name in a small circle in the middle of the space below. In various places outside this circle, write down the activities and relationships you manage. They might include work, church, family, school, kids, friends, TV watching, hobbies, and so on.

Now that you have done this, review these circles and ask yourself if each of them is actually one set of relationships or one activity or many different sets. For instance, if your kids attend multiple schools, then draw a different circle for each school. Most likely your work includes multiple groups of people with whom you must relate on a consistent basis. If your children are involved in extracurricular activities, then add circles for those. What about extended family? Your spouse's work?

A choice for simplicity might begin by eliminating one television program per week and using that time to reflect on what God is doing in your life. Or it might mean asking your kids to be involved in one less activity per year. It could also mean choosing to live closer to work instead of making long commutes or taking the bus in order to use the commute time differently.

Other choices for simplicity could mean cutting out one regular weekly purchase (eating out, clothing, or coffee) and putting that money in a jar, allowing it to accumulate over a period of three months. Then seek the Lord about how he wants you to spend the money according to his kingdom.

So many times, those who talk about simplicity do so in grandiose ways that most of us find unrelateable. The key to simplicity is not to find some huge way to be simple but to find one or two little ways to make a little more room for God in the normal actions of life and then allow the Spirit of God to take things from there. As you do this as a group, you will find time and money to love one another and the world around you in fresh ways.

Use the following space to record your reflections on this practice:

Practice: Jesus's Meal

The Lord Jesus, on the night he was betrayed, took bread, and when he had given thanks, he broke it and said, "This is my body, which is for you; do this in remembrance of me." In the same way, after supper he took the cup, saying, "This cup is the new covenant in my blood; do this, whenever you drink it, in remembrance of me." For whenever you eat this bread and drink this cup, you proclaim the Lord's death until he comes.

1 Corinthians 11:23–26

Whenever I read the above passage, my imagination immediately goes to the image of a table sitting in the front of the church sanctuary that is covered with a white cloth. Then after the preaching service, the pastor stands in front of the table and asks the deacons to come forward. And then our practice of the Lord's Supper begins.

Other traditions have much more formal experiences reenacting Jesus's last meal. Some call it communion, others the Eucharist. And with each tradition, there are various ways of properly partaking of this meal. Whatever your tradition, it is important for missional communities to think through how they will practice Jesus's meal together and determine the importance this meal plays in the life of the community of God's people.

A Meal

We have enough historical records from the New Testament and from documents outside the Bible to piece together how the early church practiced the taking of the bread and the wine. First, in the accounts of Jesus's Last Supper in Matthew, Mark, and Luke, we see that Jesus shares the bread and wine as part of a meal in the upper room of a normal house. This is not a formal religious meal in a religious setting. It is simply the last meal before his death that Jesus shares with his community. In this setting we read that he tells his closest friends that they are to eat the bread and drink the cup "in remembrance of me."

Second, the disciples are accustomed to eating with Jesus and listening to him teach or minister to those around the table while they eat. Jesus enters into the normal practices of life to demonstrate what God is like.

Third, eating with his followers is a significant part of Jesus's ministry after his resurrection. After walking on the road to Emmaus with two disciples, he blesses them and eats with them. And it is when he breaks the bread that they suddenly recognize that the resurrected Jesus is in their midst. In another instance, the resurrected Jesus cooks fish on the shore while Peter, Andrew, James, and John are fishing.

The importance of eating together seems to establish a broader context for formal instructions regarding the bread and wine that carries over into the early church. We see that believers in the Jerusalem church "broke bread in their homes" (Acts 2:46). This has long been interpreted as a reference to the formal practice of following Jesus's pattern in the last meal. In addition, the reference from Paul's first letter to the Corinthians cited above is part of a larger section that provides instruction and correction to the church when they share a meal and also take the bread and the wine (see 1 Cor. 11:17–34). Jude 12 refers to *agape feasts* that, when put beside the references in Acts and 1 Corinthians, imply that the early church experienced the Lord's Supper as part of a larger, shared meal.

So it could be said that Jesus's instruction to remember him when we take the bread and wine could be taken to mean, "Every time you gather and eat together, remember that my life, death, and resurrection is the reason that you are able to share this meal. And by remembering me in eating together, remember that I am present with you." This may seem rather simple or even sacrilegious, but it is similar to the experience of the churches in the first century.

Practice Lessons

This does not mean that we should demean Jesus's meal to the level of simply *eating together*. Instead it means that we should recognize that the common meal is actually a very spiritual act of remembering who Jesus was and is for us today. It means that we have the opportunity to include the act of eating the bread and drinking the wine as part of our meals together.

This, of course, would require that groups eat a meal together. To simply take the bread and wine without a meal in the small group ritualizes the experience and deconstructs the relational nature of experiencing Jesus around the simple act of eating together. If a group cannot share a meal every week, doing so once per month seems to be a minimum.

Those from some traditions might not feel comfortable practicing Jesus's meal in small groups. The reasons will vary, and it is not important to identify them here. There are, however, ways to incorporate a meal into the life of groups while at the same time honoring the patterns of specific traditions. For instance, some have said that the *agape meal* experienced by the early churches was actually the gathering of a few house churches where a potluck meal was shared and Jesus's meal experienced. The same could be done today with multiple groups, and a church leader could be present to lead the formal receiving of the bread and wine. Or another approach would be for a church leader to attend a group on the designated evening for receiving Jesus's meal.

The point is not that there is a *right* way to practice this rhythm of all groups for all times. The issue is that we need to determine how receiving the meal Jesus left us fits into the life of a group. He left us a meal that is to be shared around the table with people who are committed to a shared life before God. How we eat together as God's people impacts how we relate to God together. Eating together and sharing this meal can be one of the most significant acts of prayer we can do in this life.

A second-century church document called the Didache provides a simple prayer for the groups that took the bread and wine before a meal. Before taking the bread they would read the blessing of the broken bread:

> We give you thanks, our Father,
> For the life and knowledge you have made known to us
> Through Jesus, your servant.
> Just as this broken bread was scattered upon the mountains
> And then was gathered together and became one,
> So may your church be gathered together
> From the ends of the earth into your kingdom;
> For yours is the glory and the power through Jesus Christ
> forever.

Before sharing the cup, they read together:

> We give you thanks, our Father,
> For the holy vine of David your servant,

Which you have made known to us through Jesus, your
   servant;
To you be the glory forever. Amen.[11]

Questions to ponder for your group:

1. How has your church traditionally practiced communion?
2. How might the group *remember* by sharing a common meal together?
3. What has been the role of formal leadership in the practice of communion in your church?
4. What are some ways that the taking of the wine and the bread could be practiced in small groups that honors your tradition? Talk with your pastor or coach and see what creative ways arise.

Use the following space to record your reflections on this practice:

Practice: Keeping the Sabbath

Remember the Sabbath day by keeping it holy.

Exodus 20:8

If there is one rhythm that can be labeled as the most concrete practice of those who are God's people, it is the keeping of the Sabbath. The references to Sabbath are central to the creation story, the exodus story, and the resurrection story. But quite possibly this rhythm can be the one we most often ignore today in the church. There are lots of reasons we give for not seeing the value of this rhythm. In talking with a pastor about his typical week, I asked if he practiced Sabbath keeping. He responded that he did not because he loved his job so much that he did not feel the need to rest.

The issue, though, is not whether we need to rest. The issue is that of trust. Do we trust God enough to stop working for one day a week? Do we trust God enough to resist the need to produce something? In our 24/7 world, where we fall behind if any time is wasted, this is a crucial question. What does Sabbath look like in this culture? And how do we practice it when involvement in church leadership (both the paid variety and the volunteer variety) often means more activity, not less?

Listening to the Rhythm

The pattern of work for six days and rest for one is woven into the fabric of the biblical narrative. To be part of God's people is to understand the flow of work and rest. In the creation story we are told that God rested on the seventh day. In the Exodus record of the Ten Commandments, the people of God were to keep the Sabbath holy because God practiced the Sabbath in the creation and they were to follow his pattern. In the account of the Ten Commandments in Deuteronomy, the reason given for keeping the Sabbath is to remember they were delivered from slavery and are now free.

Creation and deliverance from slavery are purely gifts of God to be received; there is nothing that people can do to make either happen. Keeping the Sabbath is a rhythm that keeps us aware that God's action of creation and deliverance continues in our midst today. It is the way we train ourselves that we are not ultimately in control and that we cannot produce the things of God that matter most in this world.

Creation and deliverance are ongoing actions of God's Holy Spirit in this world, not just something we remember in the annals of history. We must develop sensitivity so we can recognize God at work in our lives and our communities. The act of seeing what God is doing is something we develop by resting; it is not something we develop by working or acting. We must learn to rest and watch God's hand,

97

and one of the ways we do this is by setting aside a day for rest, to step back from the normal activity of the other six days and look at the world from a different perspective.

Those who know how to rest in God one day per week also know how to enter his rest during the other six days. This one day prepares them for resting in God while they work. But those who do not practice Sabbath keeping cannot avoid getting caught up in the standard rhythms of this world, which are anything but restful.

Sabbath vs. Leisure

Now some might say that people today do plenty of resting. There are more leisure activities today than have ever existed in the history of mankind. Just think of all the movies, spectator sports, television programs, video games, water parks, theme parks, and vacation spots that are options in or near your city or town. Some have said that we are entertaining ourselves to death, and if that is the case, then don't we have enough rest in our lives?

Leisure rest differs from Sabbath rest. In leisure rest we escape from the world into mindless numbness. We go to the theatre to escape from the pressure cooker of this world. We watch TV or attend a football game in order to enter an alternative experience than the stresses of our everyday lives.

In the Sabbath rest we set aside a day for two reasons. First, it is a day of *not working* or not producing goods or services for the sake of personal gain or sustenance. We have six days for production; this day is about trusting God for our sustenance. Second, it is a day for asking to see what God is up to in my life, the life of my community and in my neighborhood. On this day we look at what God is doing in our world and take in God's creation by reflecting on the previous week and offering the next week to God.

Practice Lessons

Some do this while taking a walk; others do so while driving though the countryside. Some might sit alone in their room for a bit, while others might hang out with friends. Some journal, some pray quietly and reflect, and others share their heart aloud over a meal with a friend or mentor. There is no Sabbath formula.

98

In our fast-paced world, it will prove difficult to practice the Sabbath alone. If Sabbath keeping is simply something that individuals choose to do and we fail to see how it can be practiced together in our groups, we will simply fail to do it in our manic world today. This might mean that some in a group might set aside Saturday for a Sabbath or another day off because of their work schedules or their commitments to the church programs on Sunday. When group members do this together, even if on different days of the week, then each one rests not alone, full of their own personal needs, stresses, and deadlines, but they go and rest with and for one another. Their group life together will be shaped by what God is doing in their lives individually and collectively for the sake of the world. Is this practice a stretch for most of us in our culture today? Yes, it is. "No one does this," you might respond. All the more reason it should be practiced by God's people, because no one did in the time when God delivered the Israelites from Egypt either.

Use the following space to record your reflections on this practice:

7

The Rhythm of Missional Relating as a Group

Josiah Royce, an American philosopher from the twentieth century, writes, "My life means nothing, either theoretically or practically, unless I am a member of a community."[1] We often don't see community like this. We view it as an option that I choose if it benefits me as an individual. We often treat it as a commodity that we evaluate and measure to determine if it has personal value. Unless we shift this attitude toward loving others in community, we will miss a great opportunity to be on mission in this world.

Jay was one of the group leaders in my church. He called with a sense of desperation and asked if we could meet. When I arrived at his house, he told me about two men in his group who came close to getting into a fistfight after the Sunday service. I was excited to hear this. The tension had been mounting between them for a few weeks, but no one knew what to do. Their group had great potential to impact their neighborhood because it was composed of quite a mix of people, including a couple of new Christians and one or two people who were asking questions about becoming a Jesus follower. To make a long story less complicated, the two men met with a couple of other group members and worked out their differences. One quit judging the other, and one actually dealt with his aversion toward having close relationships. The group as a whole saw what transpired, which created new energy. Others outside the group became interested in the group, and people were added to it. Very quickly, one group became three.

The way we relate to one another is as important to our missional way of being in the world as anything else. Jesus told his disciples, "A new command I give you: Love one another. As I have loved you, so you must love one another. By this everyone will know that you are my disciples, if you love one another" (John 13:34–35). Among the Twelve is a Zealot and a tax collector. The Zealot is a political enemy of Rome who sought to restore Israel by force; the tax collector is a Roman sympathizer. They would have despised one another in their normal interaction. Into this group Jesus said, "The rest of the world will understand who I am when you lay aside your concern for whether you connect with one another socially and instead love those who are dramatically different from you."

As I have stated earlier, being missional is inherently relational, and relationships are messy and take time. But sometimes the simple actions of actively loving one another can have an impact on the world around us in mysterious ways we cannot explain. Here are some practices that are crucial to missional life in Western culture at this time in history:

Practice: A Primary Group

My prayer is not for them alone. I pray also for those who will believe in me through their message, that all of them may be one, Father, just as you are in me and I am in you. May they also be in us so that the world may believe that you have sent me. I have given them the glory that you gave me, that they may be one as we are one—I in them and you in me—so that they may be brought to complete unity. Then the world will know that you sent me and have loved them even as you have loved me.

John 17:20–23

These verses are part of Jesus's prayer immediately before his arrest, asking that those who become part of his movement will walk in unity. This unity of oneness will result in the world believing that Jesus was sent by the Father. It is awesome to think that the way we demonstrate God to the world is by our unity with one another.

Most of us are just managing commitments and juggling activities and relationships, and as a result, the small group becomes just another meeting on the calendar. Jesus does not see things this way. He tells his disciples that the way his followers relate to one another in their everyday lives is a mark of being his disciples (see John 13:34–35). In 1 John we read, "If we say we love God yet hate a brother or sister, we are liars. For if we do not love a fellow believer, whom we have seen, we cannot love God, whom we have not seen" (4:20).

With the overwhelming busyness of our world, often the closest we get to love is when we don't do anything harmful to others. In other words, we are just being nice. We fail to truly love because we do not take the risks of love. We actually opt out of the risk of love because we don't invest in a primary group of people who become like a family. In order to love this way, we must intentionally break the rhythms of how relationships are normally done and step out and invest ourselves in others.

We Cannot Love Everyone

We cannot invest equally or in the same way in every relationship we have. If we do, we will only give morsels of connection, which is not really love. Unless we establish a primary group, we flitter about from relationship to relationship without any depth in any of these connections. We have so many relationships that none can go to any depth.

But when there is a primary group—five to twelve people with whom we choose to share life—this group becomes a center or core group. We learn to walk together, but not necessarily because the relationships are beneficial or even advantageous. In fact, there will be times when the relationships cost much more than they offer in return. But this group provides a place for our lives to belong.

To make such a group primary, it will require rethinking how we connect with all of the various "thin" relationships in our lives. Since we cannot pour ourselves into every one, we have to choose relationships into which we will pour ourselves.

103

Practice Lessons

Here are a few things that help a group practice this rhythm:

1. COVENANT KEEPING

Covenant is a biblical concept that captures the practice of self-sacrificial, other-oriented love. But it is even more than that. It is the process of being clear about how this love will be expressed. It is the way people talk about expectations regarding how they will love one another so that they know how they will do life together. This is the reason that knowing the rhythms in this book is not enough. A group must clearly understand how they will do these rhythms together and talk about the expectations of what it means for them to be a missional group.

When a group talks about expectations and clarifies how they will love one another, they will be able to speak to what it means to be a primary group. When groups create covenants, they discuss things like how often they will meet formally, how they will make the relationships in the group a priority, how they will encourage one another, and how they will minister to others outside the group. When we talk about such things, we are not aiming to generate a list of legalistic expectations, but we seek to be clear about how we will be a group.

2. FACE-TO-FACE CONTACT

This practice would not have to be stated overtly in any generation but ours. Ours is the first that has facilitated connections through a means other than face-to-face. Now we can maintain relationships through all kinds of creative means without ever seeing one another. And while things like Facebook, email, and text messaging can help with communication, they cannot replace seeing the other person. If a group is going to develop into being primary, then being in each other's presence outside of the meeting is crucial.

This does not mean the entire group must get together. It means the group members need to learn how to relate together beyond the group meeting. Other interaction can be practiced in meeting for a meal or coffee, dropping by someone's house on the way home from work, working together on a project, and so forth. The list is as extensive as the creativity of the people in the group.

3. REPETITION OF CONTACT

Life as a primary group will be developed as group members practice small touches. Too many times we expect every encounter with a friend to be significant and time-intensive. But some of the best parts of life are found in small, short, and sometimes unplanned connections. We don't need to have long, deep conversations in order to express care. It is the repetition of small touches that builds trust and communicates the priority people have in our life.

4. OVERLAP CIRCLES

One of the best ways for a group to become primary is to include the people in the small group in some of our other circles in the Life Rhythms Diagram. A group member might be invited to a family outing. A few from the group might attend a Little League game of a kid from the group. Two men might have lunch together at one's workplace. The way we get to know other people is by seeing them in various environments. If we only see each other in small group or church services, our knowledge of each other is very limited.

5. WASTE TIME TOGETHER

Some of us know how to be present during the lows, when there is a need or an emergency. When someone dies or is in the hospital, everyone shows up. Lots of people offer their prayers and express concern. We also know how to be present during the highs and times of celebration. When things are good, people love being around us.

But what about during the normal times? This rhythm is not played during the highs and lows of life that occur here and there; it is practiced in the normal stuff of life, the everyday realities we face. A primary group knows how to waste time together, eating, laughing, taking walks, meeting for coffee, and other quite simple things that make life rich.

On a final note: For those who live in large cities, practicing the rhythm of creating a primary group is almost impossible without taking proximity into consideration. If group members have to drive more than five to ten minutes to attend a meeting, it will be almost impossible to create any kind of spontaneous life together outside of the official group meetings. Therefore, try to form a group with others who live as close to each other as possible.

Use the following space to record your reflections on this practice:

Practice: A Safe Place

But we have this treasure in jars of clay to show that this all-surpassing power is from God and not from us.

2 Corinthians 4:7

Community—I have yet to find anyone who does not want it. There is a deep longing within each of us to have a place of safety, to belong to a group of people and be able to say, "These are my people."

As a kid, there was one experience that exhibited this desire for a safe place more than any other. It occurred the first week of school. I stood in line, paid the lunch lady, took my tray of food, and walked into the room where everyone sat eating. I asked myself, "Where are my people?" "Where do I belong?" Each table had its labels: the jocks, the geeks, the outcasts, the do-gooders, and so on.

My problem was that I did not know where I belonged. I grew up in a small school. My graduating class was all of seventy-two students. Frisco, Texas, is a farming town that is a blip on a map. One of the advantages of going to a small school is the opportunities to get involved in lots of different things. So I was involved in just about every group possible—sports, Future Farmers of America, choir, the school production of *Romeo and Juliet*—and I was a geek. I was always looking for a different table because as soon as I chose one I realized that there was part of me that was not accepted at that table.

Only if a group plays the rhythm of being a safe place for people to be themselves will it be able to enter into the life and mission God intends.

Unsafe Spaces

Many groups have good intentions to create a safe place for people, but they develop practices that undermine this goal. Unsafe environments take on many different forms and basically are places where people are not free to be themselves. Following are some specific ways this is manifested.

The group that wants to fix people. In such experiences there are people who want to help others get over their pain or struggle. Instead of letting an individual come to a place of self-discovery, they want to identify their problems and explain how they can change.

The group that forces people. In the name of sharing and being transparent, this kind of group sets an expectation that people will share their struggle even if they don't feel comfortable doing so. Such forced transparency undermines the hope for openness.

The group that has the right answers. This kind of group is usually a Bible study–focused group that highly values digging into the meaning behind the Scriptures. An attitude of right and wrong can develop, and often two or three people will dominate the conversation. They think they are doing the right thing by providing the *right* information, but actually they are causing hearts to close off.

The group that has it all together. The thought that Christian maturity means the absence of personal struggle or weakness can suck the life out of a group. Conversations will not go deeper than the surface because people won't risk sharing the truth about their life.

Practice Lessons

All of these examples of unsafe spaces have something in common: trying to get the group experience *right*. They have a set of expectations or a dream of what the group should look like, and those expectations are what undermine the safety. Safety cannot be forced or manufactured; it is too alive and dynamic. Safety can only be cultivated like growing a garden. We cannot force a plant to grow; we can only create an environment that allows it to develop.

There are four ways that groups can practice the rhythm of a safe place. First, allow people to be themselves. Safety arises out of the freedom to be who we are. If there are expectations in the group— stated or unstated—people will withdraw their true selves and present themselves as close as they can to the group's expectations. In his book *The Safest Place on Earth*, Larry Crabb writes:

> Everything in spiritual community is reversed from the world's order. It is our weakness, not our competence, that moves others; our sorrows, not our blessings, that break down the barriers of fear and shame that keep us apart; our admitted failures, not our paraded successes, that bind us together in hope.
>
> A spiritual community, a church, is full of broken people who turn their chairs toward each other because they know that they cannot make it alone. These broken people journey together with their wounds and worries and washouts visible, but are able to see beyond the brokenness to something alive and good, something whole.[2]

This is a great gift in a group. There are few places in this world where people are free to allow others to see who they are—even the bad stuff. Of course, this means that group life will be messy because brokenness is messy. But this is the reality of our lives. We try to hide it, but it eventually rises up and comes out.

Second, give room for people to listen to what is going on inside themselves. In our shared life, we are to invite others to allow their soul to come out. We do this by giving each other space to see the truth for themselves. They don't need us to charge in and try to make them see something or change. God is at work in people by the power of the Spirit; we don't have to play that role. We only need to give people room to listen to what the Spirit is saying. The group can also provide feedback to what they sense, but only gently and with a sense of humility rather than judgment. When control or dominance is used to force a particular perspective on another person's soul, the result is withdrawal.

Third, we must learn to speak forgiveness and healing over one another. We become God's mouthpiece proclaiming the truth of 1 John 1:9: "If we confess our sins, he is faithful and just and will forgive us our sins and purify us from all unrighteousness." It is also how we receive our healing and restoration. The book of James tells us a simple way to receive God's healing touch: "Therefore confess your sins to each other and pray for each other so that you may be healed" (5:16).

Finally, this kind of safety is best fostered when group members do these things outside of the group meetings. Safety is about being a safe *people,* not just having safe *meetings.* Safety in a meeting requires appropriate levels of communication. When new people visit a group or certain intimate subjects require some discretion, it is best for that communication to occur in one-on-one conversations, in a subgroup that is gender specific, or just talking on the phone.

Use the following space to record your reflections on this practice:

Practice: Saying Hello

All the brothers and sisters here send you greetings. Greet one another with a holy kiss.

1 Corinthians 16:20

It might seem unnecessary to devote an entire practice to something as simple as greeting one another. But I find it interesting that the apostle Paul devotes almost an entire chapter in his most theological book, Romans, to greeting people in the church. And he instructs his readers to greet one another with intentionality. There is something significant about the way Christ followers greet one another that stands in contrast to our culture.

Forgetting How to Greet

I want to suggest that we are losing our ability to initiate relationships with one another. It seems that the more chaotic life gets, the less energy we have to simply begin a conversation with another person. We have lost the art of greeting people in such a way that demonstrates genuine interest in the other person. When most enter a social setting with people they know on a surface level, they wait for someone to come and talk to them. It sometimes feels like a high school dance where no one is asking anyone to get on the floor.

People do say hello, but many don't know what to do next. I am not sure if it is a confidence issue or a lack of skills. My guess is that it is a combination of both. I have realized that one of my roles as a pastor is to help people rediscover how to greet one another in a way that is meaningful and significant. It might sound unspiritual, but it might be one of the most spiritual things we can do in our culture.

Recognizing Christ in the Other

When Ralph Neighbour preaches, he always opens with an unusual statement: "The Christ who dwells in me greets the Christ who dwells in you." I admit that when I first heard this, I did not get it; it just sounded weird. But after reflecting on the statement, I have come to see the profound truth he seeks to communicate. With his repetition of this statement, he wants to establish the fact that we are not connected to one another directly; we are connected to each other through Jesus.

Christ is in me by way of the Holy Spirit, and Christ is in you through the Holy Spirit. When we greet one another, something spiritual is happening. The Spirit within each of us is connected in ways we cannot understand. When we practice the rhythm of greeting each other, we are seeking to align ourselves around the unity of the Spirit that already exists.

When we greet one another, in a way we are actually greeting Christ. If Jesus walked through the door right now, most of us would be all ears. We would have all kinds of questions for him. If we are in Christ, it only seems reasonable that we should have the same interest in another person that we would have if he were actually Jesus sitting next to us.

What then are some ways we can break the mold of greeting people poorly and embrace them with a genuine greeting?

Practice Lessons

Here are three basic lessons that can help foster this practice:

1. DEMONSTRATE INTEREST

Years ago I read the book *How to Win Friends and Influence People*. One thing stood out to me. Dale Carnegie writes about how he can make almost anyone feel connected by simply asking them questions about their interests. He lists six ways to connect with people after saying hello:

1. Become genuinely interested in other people.
2. Smile.
3. Remember that a person's name is to that person the sweetest and most important sound in any language.
4. Be a good listener. Encourage others to talk about themselves.
5. Talk in terms of the other person's interests.
6. Make the other person feel important—and do it sincerely.[3]

The fact is that everyone likes to talk about themselves, and if you take the initiative and ask questions about the other person's interests, it will insert a small act of love into the conversation. This may seem insignificant or a small act of kindness, but think about it: When was the last time someone showed genuine interest in you and what you like to talk about? How did it make you feel? What did you think about the person after the conversation?

The problem, though, is that many small groups assume that the focus should be on deep spiritual issues. They look for deep sharing and transparent communication as a sign of genuine spiritual connection. And while that is important, most people will not open up their hearts unless you are willing to also hear about some of

111

the insignificant things in life. Whether it's sports, a favorite television show, a new restaurant that opened, or just what happened at work, sharing personal interests is an important part of greeting one another properly.

This is the reason icebreakers are so important to a small group meeting. Few people are ready to share what they think, much less how they feel, about spiritual issues unless they first feel that someone has listened to them about something less intense. And besides that, whoever said that laughter, telling stories, and sharing interests is not spiritual? In our world, where many people don't have time to interact about such things, conversations like this can be quite spiritual.

2. LISTEN WELL

A second-century Roman philosopher once said, "Nature gave us two ears and one tongue so we could listen twice as much as we speak." While this is true, unfortunately most of us are thinking more about what we are planning to say next instead of focusing on what the other person is actually saying. We are letting the other person talk, while waiting for an opportunity to insert our perspective.

In his book *Seven Habits of Highly Effective People*, Steven Covey puts it this way: "Seek first to understand and then to be understood." If this principle is core to relationships in the business world, it is even more crucial to our communication with one another in community. But too often every group member comes to any gathering full of his or her need to be heard, not to listen. In greeting one another, we need to slow down and actually choose to engage the other person and focus on him or her. Imagine if an entire group practiced this rhythm week after week; how would it increase the value these people have for the group?

This kind of listening must be intentional and active. Researchers on communication recognize four characteristics of good listeners. They:

1. Desire to be *other-directed*, rather than to project one's own feelings and ideas onto the other.
2. Desire to be *nondefensive*, rather than to protect the self. When the self is being protected, it is difficult to focus on the other person.

3. Desire to *imagine the roles, perspectives, or experiences of the other*, rather than assuming they are the same as one's own.
4. Desire to listen as a *receiver, not as a critic*, and desire to understand the other person rather than to achieve either agreement from or change in that person.[4]

3. Have Fun

Groups that know how to laugh together know how to cry together. Groups that carve out time for sharing food, playing a board game, or just sitting around telling stories will be groups that have the ability to connect on deeper levels. Show me the group that is serious all of the time, and I will show you a group that will eventually wear people out.

Some might respond to this dogmatic statement with a claim that the group is just serious in nature. But if that is the case, I propose that this group is the one that needs to laugh the most. They need to do something that will help them loosen up and take things a little less seriously. The world is ominous enough; the last thing we need in the church are groups that are adding to that heaviness.

The fruit of the Spirit is *joy*. When we relate to one another in and through Christ, the Spirit will bring joy to these relationships. The pressure lifts and we can simply relate and see where the relationship goes.

Use the following space to record your reflections on this practice:

Practice: Pressing through Conflict

But to you who are listening I say: Love your enemies, do good to those who hate you, bless those who curse you, pray for those who mistreat

113

you. If someone slaps you on one cheek, turn the other also. If someone takes your coat, do not withhold your shirt. Give to everyone who asks you, and if anyone takes what belongs to you, do not demand it back. Do to others as you would have them do to you.

If you love those who love you, what credit is that to you? Even sinners love those who love them. And if you do good to those who are good to you, what credit is that to you? Even sinners do that. And if you lend to those from whom you expect repayment, what credit is that to you? Even sinners lend to sinners, expecting to be repaid in full. But love your enemies, do good to them, and lend to them without expecting to get anything back. Then your reward will be great, and you will be children of the Most High, because he is kind to the ungrateful and wicked. Be merciful, just as your Father is merciful.

Luke 6:27–36

Being one of Jesus's followers means we learn to practice a radical kind of life. We are to love our enemies—those who hate, curse, and mistreat us. Little disrupts our lives like enemies, and yet enemies abound in our world. Threats of terrorists, countries with whom we go to war, a political party that opposes our agenda, those at work who undermine us—these are the expected enemies, the obvious ones whom we are called to love and see as having value and worth before God.

These are enemies at a distance; most of us don't actually know any of them except through the news. But there is another kind of enemy that we do know and we don't expect. These are the up-close enemies. We often don't realize our up-close friends can become our enemies, and therefore we don't realize how we need to treat them.

The Up-Close Enemy

This kind of enemy is discovered through the actions of hatred from a good friend, the cursing from your coworker, or the mistreatment from your spouse. These are the enemies we can potentially face every day. They might include:

- the coworker who got the commission you deserved;
- the spouse who stands against you rather than for you;

114

- the friend who doesn't have time for you anymore; or
- the child who won't obey.

These are your unexpected enemies, and you will find such enemies in group life also.

There is common teaching about how groups develop in stages. These stages are Forming, Storming, Norming, Performing, and Reforming. These stages describe the common experience of how group life moves through time. The way different groups do it will vary, but the pattern is the same.

This first stage of Forming identifies how groups begin around superficial relationships in which individuals protect their self-interest and question what is going on. Everything is new and exciting, but there are usually questions and apprehensions. After the Forming comes the Storming, or the conflict stage of the group. This is when people begin to see reality as they learn about each other. Weaknesses come to light. People are disappointed. Someone hurts another person. A member leaves the meeting because he or she is upset. Here is a time when group members can feel like enemies toward each other.

If a group is willing to work through the Storming, they enter the Norming or Community stage. This is when the group members begin to accept each other and work to support one another more naturally. This is usually followed by the Performing stage. I say *usually* because many groups don't make it this far. But for those who do, they find that the group begins to spontaneously minister together both to each other and to those outside the group.

The final stage is Reforming. This occurs when the Lord leads a group in a new direction.

Most people want to experience the Norming and Performing stages, but few realize that these only come on the other side of the Storm. We must practice the rhythm of working through the conflict. If we do this in the church, we will definitely stand out in our culture because we live in a culture that does not know how to do conflict that well.

Reflex Reactions

When an enemy hurts you, steals from you, interrupts your plans, or stands against you, you have a natural knee-jerk reaction. You don't even think about it. In most situations these reactions are culturally acceptable. Few would question your right to fight back, run away, or complain about it to others. That is just the way things are done.

Because members of groups don't think through how they will handle conflict, they fall into the pattern of the world. They fight one another, run away, or complain to people outside the groups. As a result, a lot of groups bounce back and forth between Forming and Storming. They like one another, but when someone acts like an enemy, they back off so they don't have to deal with the situation. And then when the issue has been fully swept under the rug, they like one another again. This is a great recipe for maintaining surface relationships. This can be especially bad in churches where there is a church culture that expects everyone to be nice all the time.

Group life would be much easier if everyone would just treat each other the way God wants us to. But that is just not reality. Every group, every friendship, every marriage is going to face the reality that someone in the relationship will act like an enemy. And if the one who is hurt responds in kind or runs away, nothing is ever really faced.

In Luke 6:32–34 Jesus challenges us by saying: What credit is it to you if you . . .

love those who love you?

do good to those who do good to you?

lend to those who have the ability to lend to you in the future?

Even sinners live that well. But we are called to love others even when it is not to our benefit, even when they have hurt us and cursed us. So what does this look like?

Practice Lessons

When we are getting to know one another, inevitably someone will say something that offends another. Most of the time the speaker doesn't mean it in the way it is received, but if the one who is hurt enters into a pattern of pain, judgment, and condemnation, it will

116

be very difficult to find reconciliation. How do we then establish a different practice of love in the midst of conflict?

1. *To love like this requires faith.* When another person in my group hurts me, I have to trust that God is at work in him or her. I have to look to God so that I can assume the best about the other person and resist judgment and condemnation. So much of the conflict that groups face relates to communication differences. Different personalities communicate in different ways.

2. *To love like this requires intentionality.* We must prepare ourselves for how we are going to do conflict. If we don't, then we will just live in the world of our knee-jerk reactions. The entire group must be committed to working it through. This means that the people in the group must stay put. No one can just opt out because they are uncomfortable or they don't like the group anymore. This does not mean permanence, but too often group members leave because they have an easy-out approach to group life.

3. *To love like this requires creativity.* There is no list of rules of what to do and not do in order to love. That is not how love works. Jesus simply instructs us to:
   - do good,
   - bless,
   - pray for our enemies,
   - give without expecting the other person to give back to you.

Eugene Peterson translates Luke 6:31 like this: "Ask yourself what you want people to do for you; then grab the initiative and do it for them!" (Message). This does not mean that the one who is being hurt becomes a doormat or victim and lets the hurt continue. Instead it means that the one who is hurt is willing to risk telling the truth about how he or she was hurt and work through the implications of that.

To love in this way is a result of the work of the Spirit. The Holy Spirit's fruit is "love, joy, peace, patience, kindness, goodness, faithfulness, gentleness and self-control" (Gal. 5:22–23). Notice how all of these are relational words. The fruit of the Spirit does not address my inner sense of spiritual well-being. God's work in me and my group is manifest in the way we relate to each other. In conflict, we call on God to manifest the Spirit's fruit. Without this, a group will get stuck in the hurt, logic, and anxiety of individuals within the group. But when God brings a group through conflict, the members begin to love truly and in reality. And this is distinctively of God.

Use the following space to record your reflections on this practice:

Practice: Build Up Each Other

Knowledge puffs up, but love builds up.

1 Corinthians 8:1 NIV

The Greek word for "build up" is *oikodomeo*, which means to edify, to encourage, to cause to grow. In chapter 14 of the same letter, Paul uses the word *oikodomeo* six times, emphasizing the fact that the purpose of spiritual gifts, the movement of the Holy Spirit in the church, is to edify the body. In Greek, *oikodomeo* is related to the word *oikos*, which means house or household. In English, *edification* is connected to the word *edifice*. One who edifies is actually building an edifice around another person. When someone has been edified, he has a spiritual house built around him to protect him from the lies of the enemy. When he has not been edified by others, he lacks that wall of protection from the enemy and is much more likely to fall prey to the enemy's traps.

118

"But everyone who prophesies speaks to men for their strengthening [edification], encouragement and comfort" (1 Cor. 14:3 NIV). God speaks through the members of his body to other body parts to generate *oikodomeo*. The rhythm of speech in our culture is far from that of building up. We have been trained in warped patterns of speech that can actually inflict harm on others in our small group experiences. As a result of this, we often speak to one another thinking we are playing the rhythm of edification when it is actually something else. I have observed some harmful patterns that we commonly play in our relationships:

1. *Flattery.* Telling people what they want to hear in their flesh is not prophecy that leads to edification. It is a way of getting people to like you by telling them that they are okay just the way they are. A few months ago, I confessed to my group that I was worried about my future. Other group members told me that it was a good idea to be concerned about providing for my family's future. I started to feel flattered until I realized that I had not confessed that I was *concerned*. They did not hear that I was not in a place of trusting God with my future. At that point, I asked the group to not let me off the hook and to challenge me to change.

2. *Swapping experiences.* John, a new group member, shared that he struggles with the desire for alcohol. Bill responded, "Yeah, I used to struggle with that too. There were times when I lay awake all night thinking about the taste of another drink. Then I started thinking about the parties I went to. At one party I drank so much that I . . ." By the time Bill finished, John and the rest of the group were lost in the details of Bill's reminiscences, and John was far from edified.

3. *Giving advice.* A woman shared with her small group that she was depressed. Another member piped up, "Last year I was depressed, and I listened to a Jaci Velasquez song and it turned me around. I'll get you a copy of that CD." Telling people what they should do is not edifying. What God used in one time and place to change a person is rarely what he uses for someone else.

4. *Quoting Scripture.* A man shared his struggles with impure thoughts. Another man stared him in the eye and said, "For-

nicators and adulterers will not inherit the kingdom of God" (see 1 Cor. 6:9). Another man shared that he lacks faith, and someone piped up, "The Bible tells us that 'without faith it is impossible to please God'" (Heb. 6:11). Such an approach tells transparent people, "I don't really know how to help you. Just read the Word and figure it out on your own."

Practice Lessons

In Larry Crabb's excellent book *SoulTalk*, he lays out the difference between *SelfTalk* and *SoulTalk*—the term he uses for prophetic edification. The harmful practices listed above are variations of SelfTalk. Crabb writes, "Without seeing Christ's life within us, our choices are either authentic SelfTalk (say what you really feel and risk destroying relationships and harming souls) or socialized SelfTalk (spin what you feel into courteous conversation and preserve shallow relationships that keep everyone's soul pleasant and empty)."[5]

SoulTalk is a rhythm of being honest and transparent without trying to fix one another. It occurs in a group where people have learned to play the rhythm in an atmosphere of safe love. When people embrace SoulTalk in a small group, they enter into the rhythm of edification by the power of God's Spirit in us. Crabb's book discusses the following stages that are needed for a group to enter this rhythm:

1. Think Beneath: When someone begins to share their need, most of the time they are sharing things that are not the root issues. To enter into spiritual edification, the group must learn to listen beneath the words, to think beneath the problems and to identify the unseen battle in the person's soul. Last week in my group, one person began sharing how he disagreed with one of the points we were trying to emphasize. At first I tried to show him that I was right and he was wrong. Then I realized that what he was saying was not the real issue at all. The root problem was that he was dealing with some latent insecurity issues that caused him to see things a little differently. When I began to think beneath his words, I led the group to stop trying to figure out his problem. We then began to see that God

was moving in his heart at much deeper levels that could not be addressed in one discussion or group meeting.

2. Think Vision: Many times we think the point of edification is to help people get over their problems and become *successful* Christians. This is not God's vision at all. If I am going to minister to my friend in my group, I have to think vision and see what God is doing in his life. Even though my friend might open up his heart in order to get over the pain, God wants to lead him through the pain and bring my friend into a new place of intimacy with him.

3. Think Passion: When I try to minister to a person who reveals a need, I must first realize that I have to get over myself and my need to be seen as the one who does the ministry. I have to get over my ego so it cannot get in the way of showing some-one real love. Crabb writes, "But you must see your own mess clearly before you'll be able to see the mess in another person's soul with clarity and without judgment."[6] Every time I sense the Spirit's edifying word through me, it has been after first realizing that I don't know what to say or do. I hit a wall that causes me to wait on God and listen to him. When I fail to wait, I might offer some advice or some other form of SelfTalk, but it lacks power to change lives.

4. Think Story: Part of edification is allowing the other people in the room to share their stories. We must ask inviting ques-tions that will open doors for them to open up, because most people are reluctant to reveal the life-shaping events of their lives. It requires effort to create an environment that is safe enough for people to share more than their successes but also their struggles, failures, and faults; in other words, to be a real person. Many times when people are given the space to tell their stories, they discover for themselves what God is saying. This is even more powerful than being told a specific truth.

5. Think Movement: The Spirit is at work in the person who shares a need. The job of the edifier is to discover what the Spirit is doing and then begin to move in that direction. It is a movement of leading people to a deeper sense of dependency, intimacy, and love for God. It is a movement of revelation and change, one of repenting of how we see God and see ourselves. It is not

a movement of fixing people's problems or finding ten steps to a successful and fulfilled life. It is a dance of mystery.

Crabb warns, "There are some things we can understand, some truths we can know because God revealed them to us in the Bible. But what we can know will never serve as a manual for helping people change. Mystery will always exceed knowledge. There's no formula for SoulTalk, but if there were, it would be ten parts mystery to one part knowledge. Did we really think it would be different?"[7] We cannot manipulate the Spirit's movement and make this rhythm happen. It is simply a part of what God is doing through his people, and one of the marks of God's people is that they learn how to sing or play this song along with him. We can only seek him in the dance.

Use the following space to record your reflections on this practice:

Practice: Family Life and Small Groups

He called a little child, whom he placed among them. And he said: "Truly I tell you, unless you change and become like little children, you will never enter the kingdom of heaven. Therefore, whoever takes a humble place—becoming like this child—is the greatest in the kingdom of heaven. And whoever welcomes one such child in my name welcomes me."

Matthew 18:2–5

The question of children adds a whole layer of complexity to group life. Groups that have kids usually have a lot of them because parents with children have a lot in common. It is not unusual for a small group with four couples to have twelve to fifteen children. People want to know, "What do we do with the kids?"

But the question about family is much bigger than whether kids are present and what to do with them while the adults meet. The question is really about how group life connects with the family. If a small group is to become a primary group, there is the issue of how that group relates to the families of the individual members of the group. So if we want to properly understand how the children relate to group life, we must first start with this larger question.

How We Know Each Other

Look again at the Life Rhythm Diagram on page 31. If you are like most people, each circle of activities and relationships often requires something different of you. Each of the groups represented by these circles are independent of one another. But if I were to truly get to know you, I would need to interact with you in a few of your circles, not just one. But for most of us, this is simply not possible, so we have to think through how we will get to know one another outside of group activities.

One of the best ways to do this is by spending time together with your immediate families. If you want to know who I am, interact with me as I relate to my wife and kids. If you only connect with me alone, you will only get part of me. The same is true with my parents. If you see me interact with them, you will see parts of me that do not come out in any other context.

This does not mean that a group needs to encompass three generations in order to create true connections. I am simply saying that the more a group interacts with the generation above and the generation below, the more they will know and connect with one another. I realize that this goes against the grain of our culture, and to be quite honest, it goes against the way the church in America has done small groups. Most of us think about our group as one of our circles, and family relationships need not overlap. There is something almost mystical, however, that occurs with regard to the depth of connections when there is even the smallest interaction with other family members. The whole person begins to come out, and connections begin to occur that cannot be explained.

Practice Lessons

While there are practical ways to make inclusion of the children in group life doable, addressing the practical issues is minor by comparison to a much bigger barrier that hinders effective kid inclusion. Most of the time the biggest issue with regard to the kids is the attitude of group members. (Interestingly enough, as I wrote this last sentence, a little six-year-old boy came to my table at the coffee shop to see what I was doing on the computer.)

Oftentimes, group members see the children in a way that is counterproductive. Some of these ways include these false beliefs:

- Kids are a nuisance to group life.
- Small groups are for adults, and the kids are not group members until they can participate in the discussion.
- Spiritual things are serious and intense.
- Bible study is the purpose of the meeting and it is an intellectual activity.
- Kids are not old enough to be used by the Spirit.

Most people don't verbalize such beliefs or attitudes, but they are present. Honestly, I have yet to find a group with children that does not deal with these issues. In our world we are taught that there are adult activities and there are children's activities, and the two do not necessarily intertwine.

The small group can provide a venue where the family can be set within a wider primary group and the kids find a sense of belonging beyond their parents. The kids begin to connect with other adults and "aunts" and "uncles" and might even eventually lean on them to talk about issues they are not comfortable discussing with their parents. Such an experience underscores the old adage that it takes a village to raise a child.

But this requires some shifts in thinking about how the children participate in the life of the group:

1. Every child must be viewed as a full member of the group, not just the child of a member. This means that the adults must learn to greet and interact with the children and welcome

them into the life of the group rather than just focus on the adults. If the kids do not feel they are part of the group, they will be more troublesome. But if they feel that they are full members, they will actually take great joy in attending the group meetings.

2. Where appropriate, allow kids age ten and over to participate in the group discussion. They can even join in on the discussions and some of the prayer time.

3. Even four-year-olds can join in on the icebreakers and some of the worship.

4. Expect interruptions. Every group meeting that includes children will have some interruptions. That is just life with kids. In our traditional Bible study mentality, we have operated from the assumption that the discussion must be focused and intellectual in order to be effective. But if the group meeting is part of our life, then any Bible discussion can occur even when there are interruptions. Just keep on going, dealing with the issue. God is still in the midst of the group because he is alive in the midst of us.

5. Don't be afraid to get help if you need it. There are many options such as hiring a babysitter, rotating who watches the children, and trading watching the kids with another group. There is also some good curriculum for kids that can promote community among them.

6. Take a break from the kids at least once per month. Mix up the pattern. Don't get in a rut. Variety is the spice of life.

7. Talk about it. One of the keys to effectively incorporating family life into group life is to discuss what you want. Work through the expectations, how discipline will happen, and the house rules of the host. It is essential to talk through these things up front because issues will arise, and when they do, these conversations will have established parameters for potentially more difficult conversations down the road.

Even though including the kids in group life can be a challenge, they can add to the fun of the group. There is something about kids that teaches us about life and about Jesus; just their presence reveals

125

something about the mystery of God. Maybe this is why Jesus said what he did about embracing them.

Use the following space to record your reflections on this practice:

Practice: Initiation into the Community

Then Jesus came to them and said, "All authority in heaven and on earth has been given to me. Therefore go and make disciples of all nations, baptizing them in the name of the Father and of the Son and of the Holy Spirit, and teaching them to obey everything I have commanded you. And surely I am with you always, to the very end of the age."

Matthew 28:18–20

When you think about it, the act of baptism is quite unusual. If you join a club in high school or become a member of a professional organization, the induction usually comes in the form of a certificate or badge of some kind. When you enter into life as God's child, the New Testament makes it quite clear that a cleansing with water is the initiation rite of passage.

Like communion, baptism is a controversial topic among church traditions. The questions about how baptism should happen, what the appropriate age for baptism is, who qualifies for baptism, and how much training should be given before baptism are all important questions. But that is far beyond the scope of this short meditation. Instead of talking about the technicalities of baptism, let's look at what baptism is and understand how it relates to the life in missional community.

Baptized "Into" God

In the passage quoted above, Jesus does not just tell his disciples to baptize. He tells them to baptize people in the name of the Father, Son, and Holy Spirit. For those who have been around the church for any length of time, these words may have lost their meaning because they have become so commonplace. But for us to understand what baptism is, we must realize that these words reveal the mystery of what it means for groups to play the rhythm of baptism.

We are baptized *into* the life of the Father, Son, and Spirit. Another way of putting it is that we are immersed in the life of God, into the eternal relationships of the three persons of the Trinity. As stated earlier, when we say *Trinity*, we are at the same time saying *love*, for "God is love." Therefore, baptism is a sign of being immersed in the love and life of God. As we are immersed in God, we join Christ in his death and our old self dies. And the immersion in God (or God's love) empowers us to rise with Christ and live a new life (see Rom. 6:2–4).

Baptism and the Way of Salvation

The New Testament clearly links the initial salvation experience with baptism. Against this there is no argument. The nature of salvation, however, seems to be substantially different today from that of the believers in the first century. In the modern imagination, people often view salvation as something that happens to individuals when they adopt a certain set of beliefs. If individuals *believe* the right things, then they are saved and are baptized into this belief system.

Jesus, Paul, and the other New Testament writers speak of salvation as being saved from a way of life so that we can live in a new way of life. Consider Paul's words in his second letter to the Corinthians:

So from now on we regard no one from a worldly point of view. Though we once regarded Christ in this way, we do so no longer. Therefore, if anyone is in Christ, the new creation has come: The old has gone, the new is here! All this is from God, who reconciled us to himself through Christ and gave us the ministry of reconciliation: that God was reconciling the world to himself in Christ, not counting people's sins against them.

5:16–19

While Paul does not use the word *salvation*—instead he speaks of *reconciliation*—the concept is the same. We are reconciled to God to enter a new way and leave the old way. It is important to notice that the personal pronouns in this passage are plural, not singular or individualistic. In other words, God did not reconcile a bunch of individuals to have individualistic relationships with him. He reconciled a people who together stand before God. Reconciliation is not about individuals having the right belief system but about a people who are lined up and living according to the ways of God. And the only way to do this is to do it together.

Baptism serves as the act of initiation for the newly reconciled into God's people. If we are baptized into Father, Son, and Spirit, we are initiated into the life of community—God's three-person community. And because of the cross, Jesus's followers are given the right to enter into this community with God. Therefore, to be baptized is not just about personal salvation; it is just as much about entering into the life and vision of the church.

Practice Lessons

Every church tradition must wrestle with baptism in order to determine the way that fits them the best. I am not going to weigh in on child baptism versus adult, dipping verses sprinkling, the kind of class required before baptism, or whether the baptizer must be an ordained minister. I do have convictions about all of these, but I also recognize other points of view are valid.

Churches of North America, however, must think through the context in which we commonly practice baptism. We must consider the meaning of the popular practice of baptism, which is performed by ordained clergy and occurs in a formal meeting, in a formal service, and before a crowd. Often the baptismal candidate is barely known by the crowd that is watching and the clergy performing the baptism has little relationship with the person. What if instead the person who shared Christ with the new believer performed the baptism and it was held in a more intimate setting with a small group who knew the person quite well? Some of the most moving baptismal services I have experienced were held in a backyard pool where the small group leader baptized the candidate. In addition to the group members present, friends and neighbors from the community came, and the baptismal act became a witness to the community, primarily because it was held in the neighborhood instead of in a formal church building.

When people are baptized in such a setting, the group takes responsibility for the person and walks with them to equip them in the ways of salvation. This goes far beyond what a baptism class can offer. The small group actually provides the context for learning to do life according to the rhythms of God.

For some church traditions, taking such a bold step is simply too radical. If you are not ready to empower groups to baptize, how then might the rite of baptism be given back to the community? Is it possible for the person who shared Christ with the candidate to participate at some level? Is there a way to have the small group come around the candidate as a part of the baptism ceremony?

When we reconsider the way we practice baptism, we are doing much more than simply doing baptism differently. We are actually confronting the individualism and isolation of our culture and how it has taken over the way we view salvation. We are showing our neighbors and friends that God's salvation is not just about making individuals better people or preparing individuals for a future in heaven, and we are actually choosing to live in a different way and go beyond a commitment to a specific set of beliefs.

Use the following space to record your reflections on this practice:

The Rhythm of Missional Engagement with the Neighborhood

Admittedly, Missional Engagement is where the action is. When envisioning missional small groups, many immediately think of the things covered in this chapter. These are active, result-oriented, measurable, and exciting ways to demonstrate the kingdom of God in this world. But those who jump into this rhythm without considering how the first two rhythms shape our lives as a people who are distinctively God's soon find that Missional Engagement loses its sustaining power. The need for availability directly impacts our need to simplify our lives. The call to do Missional Engagement together requires that we actually do life together. The symbiotic relationship among the three rhythms reinforce one another for Missional Engagement around us.

I have heard stories about missionaries most of my life. Although overly simplistic, these stories of missionaries to other countries reveal two different approaches to how they ministered. In the first approach, the missionary goes with a clear vision and a plan for reaching people. In the second approach, the missionaries begin their ministry by listening to the people. They listen for their pains, their joys, and their needs. Then they pray. Sometimes they are led to pray for a miracle, other times they pray for the means to meet a practical need, and sometimes they are led to simply engage the people in further conversation. As they listen, the Good News of Jesus rises up and becomes real in specific situations.

What if we trained groups to engage their neighborhoods with this kind of imagination? I know of a woman who moved into an underresourced neighborhood and began interacting with and baking cookies for her neighbors—who happened to be of a different nationality. She simply listened to their pain and their desires and then sought out ways to talk about what Jesus is doing in the world to change things. From this she got to know her neighbors, and through those conversations an interest in a small group arose. This group is comprised of people who most likely would not attend a Sunday service, but they are trying to figure out what it means to follow Jesus in their world.

Groups need practical ways to put this rhythm into place. In our insulated world we are cut off from our neighbors on our streets. We need ways to break through the insulation and self-protection. We need ways to do this together, not ways that simply tell individuals who feel called to "reach people for Christ."

Practice: Moving into the Neighborhood

The Word became flesh and made his dwelling among us. We have seen his glory, the glory of the one and only [Son], who came from the Father, full of grace and truth.

John 1:14

I love the way Eugene Peterson paraphrases this verse:

The Word became flesh and blood, and moved into the neighborhood. We saw the glory with our own eyes, the one-of-a-kind glory, like Father, like Son, generous inside and out, true from start to finish.

John 1:14 Message

When I think about Jesus being Immanuel, "God with us," I have always imagined this in universal terms, that God is with us in the person of Jesus for the sake of the entire world. And while Jesus came for the sake of the world, he did this in a very local way. He entered a specific neighborhood. His primary ministry was to Galilee, and there he manifested the glory of God. He did not take on the entire world in his ministry. He was a local minister.

To be in a neighborhood is to be relational. And to be relational is to be present. If we start with the way God demonstrates his life to the world and the implications that has on the way we engage the world and do evangelism, then small groups and community life will be likewise shaped. Missional Engagement is not primarily about *getting people saved*. It has more to do with demonstrating God's life together than it has to do with many of the evangelism models that have shaped the way we share Jesus's gospel.

Getting Converts

When I hear the word *evangelism*, I immediately think about a friend who called me when I lived in Houston. He and his wife wanted to take me to lunch. He was not a good friend, but I was honored by the invitation, so much so that I was willing to forego watching the Dallas Cowboys game. While eating lunch with him, I soon realized that he had a message to share with me. He had just been to a multilevel marketing conference, and before returning to his home in North Texas, he wanted to give me the opportunity to get in on this great money-making venture. He was excited about what he was sharing; to him it was good news. But all I could think about was the fact that I was missing the Cowboys game. I have never heard from him since.

Later I realized that my reaction was very similar to that of the people I had previously forced to listen to me share about Jesus. Our group had made a regular habit of eating at a Lebanese restaurant. A few of us ate there at least once a week, and we befriended the family who owned it. The son invited a couple of us to go fishing. During lunch after we caught nothing, my Christian friend awkwardly tried to tell the restaurant owner about Jesus. It was not a conversation; he had entered a monologue that was obviously uncomfortable. No invitations followed after that because we were communicating that we wanted new recruits, not friendship.

All of the research confirms that people primarily come to life in Christ through significant relationships. This principle has been applied to small groups. Members are taught to develop strategic relationships with people so they can lead them to Christ and include them in the small group. Like a salesperson who builds a relationship with someone to make the big sale, too many Christians are only befriending people so they can include them and the group can grow. I don't see this as being the approach Jesus took. Jesus moved into the neighborhood and stayed. He met them on their turf. He listened and ate with people. He was up to something much bigger and more beautiful than trying to simply add people to groups.

Before Our Neighbors

For far too long evangelism has been isolated from the other aspects of church life. It is as if we see outreach as something that is extraneous to worship, discipleship, and community. But this way of viewing evangelism is based on the assumption that we must divide the church up into a certain number of functions (evangelism being one of them) and then isolate each of those functions so they can be improved. This is the very reason I have chosen to not call this third section of the book "Missional Evangelism."

Instead it is "Missional Engagement," because God sends his people to engage a local context with the way they live. The way of life that leads to Missional Engagement is defined by the Missional Communion and Missional Relating practiced by God's people. The key is doing Missional Communion and Missional Relating before those in the neighborhood as opposed to doing it as a task that comes after Missional Communion and Relating are complete. In other words, we do all at the same time instead of breaking them up into tasks.

This approach to Missional Engagement (and thereby evangelism) is more organic than programmatic. Of course, we intentionally practice certain rhythms, but we are not creating a strategy for the purpose of winning people to Jesus or to grow our small group. Instead we practice these rhythms because that is just how the people of God are called to live. The practice of presence simply calls us to live our rhythms in the midst of others who do not know or understand why we live the way we do.

The Necessity of Working Together

In Luke 10 Jesus set an example for us by sending the disciples out in pairs. Small groups establish a presence in the neighborhood by practicing the rhythms of Missional Communion and Missional Relating so that others can see the reality of God in and through them. This is best done together. There are plenty of examples of entrepreneurial and creative individuals who caught a radical vision and accomplished it. Whether working in underresourced communities, with former convicts, with battered women, or with overworked suburbanites, every creative way of engaging these groups missionally took off only after a team of people began to live the vision together. An individual cannot do this alone. Being present is best done by two or more people so they can demonstrate how they live together in front of others.

When we practice presence in the neighborhood, we give people the opportunity to *feel* the life of the gospel and not just hear it. If we are not present in the neighborhood, we have no credibility to do some of the more proactive rhythms identified in the next few chapters. And if we are not present, we have no right to expect people to take the message of the gospel seriously. Presence establishes us as people who live in this world and as people who have a God who can do something about what is going on in this world.

Practice Lessons

Practically speaking, this requires the community that is living the rhythms of Missional Communion and Missional Relating to demonstrate availability to the neighborhood. Expressing availability is much different from being willing to help when asked or being helpful during a time of tragedy. Almost any person in our culture today responds to these situations. But what is distinctively Christian about availability is that it takes a risk to be present in the neighborhood before any need arises.

This requires those living missional rhythms to be with people where they are. It requires us to go to them and show them the life, as opposed to waiting for them to come to us when they hit an awareness of some kind of spiritual need. Alan Roxburgh identifies some

135

of the following as practical venues for engaging the neighborhood with our presence:

- Over the back fence or across the front lawn
- In stores or on the street
- Around bus stops or natural gathering places
- On the sports field with other moms and dads
- Volunteering in Scouts, Big Brothers or Sisters, hospitals, and so on
- Service clubs such as Toastmasters, Lions, Kiwanis, Rotary, and Jaycees
- Special-interest societies such as drama groups, philatelist society, literary society, music society, hiking club, cycling, bird watching, kayaking, and scuba diving
- Groups for our children in sports, music, art, and so on
- Sports for ourselves such as indoor soccer, volleyball, softball, badminton, basketball, ultimate Frisbee, BMX, and so on
- Clubs for lawyers, engineers, and other professions
- Civic activities such as political associations, civic subcommittees, and so on

This list is not meant to be exhaustive, but it is illustrative. As individuals think through these various means of engaging the neighborhood, the next step is to share this with their small group community. This allows the group to enter into the conversation and ask the question: How can we support you or do this with you? For instance, if a group member feels led to be a Big Brother, the group can ask how they can support or participate in what this individual is being led to do.

Where can your group enter the neighborhood? What are some natural points of connection and relationships that you can cultivate? If nothing immediately comes to mind, start with your street. Get to know your neighbors and see what conversations arise.

Use the following space to record your reflections on this practice:

Practice: Focus

After this the Lord appointed seventy-two others and sent them two by two ahead of him to every town and place where he was about to go. He told them, "The harvest is plentiful, but the workers are few. Ask the Lord of the harvest, therefore, to send out workers into his harvest field. Go! I am sending you out like lambs among wolves. Do not take a purse or bag or sandals; and do not greet anyone on the road."

Luke 10:1–4

Jesus sends out seventy-two of his followers to share the Good News that the kingdom has come. But this sending is not unspecified or random; it is focused and directive. Jesus sends them to the places he is about to go. His disciples are preparing the ground for his coming.

Missional Engagement is practiced as a community of people focused on being present in a specific time and place. It is about living in the local and being focused on doing the small stuff of the kingdom for a specific group of people so they can actually experience and *feel* the life of Christ in and through the community.

Stories That Mislead

Most of the stories shared about evangelism and missions are spectacular. A conference speaker relates how he shared Christ with someone on the plane and a sudden, immediate transformation occurred. A preacher tells of a waitress who wants to come to church after he left a very large tip and asked how her life was going. A missionary reports sharing the gospel with a tribal group who had no exposure to Jesus or the Bible. These are exciting stories, and

137

there is nothing wrong with them except for the fact that they are so exciting that they often create a view of sharing Jesus with the world that most cannot do. Most of God's people do not fly on planes, preach at a church, or engage tribal people. Most of us are just normal people who talk about everyday things with regular people.

What we need are stories about engaging these people with the gospel so that the entire church can envision how sharing Jesus occurs in real life. How about going bowling as a group and inviting a neighbor to enjoy the evening with you? Or spending time with a coworker over lunch to listen to what is going on in his or her life? Or mowing your neighbor's yard just because?

The first set of stories create an imagination of sharing Jesus that is random and universal. Every person you meet is a potential candidate to receive Jesus. But in all three examples in the second set, there is an assumption of an ongoing conversation that requires the development of focused, loving relationships. They are not random acts of kindness with whoever walks by; they are acts of kindness for people we know.

The Mission Field Has Shifted

Over the last three hundred years, when people talked about missions, they meant doing ministry in a foreign country or starting a new church in America for those who did not speak English. The assumption was that the West was Christianized and the rest of the world was not. So the task of the church was to do missions overseas and simply tell the unchurched in the West about Jesus so they could pray a prayer and join a church. But we can no longer rightly say that the West is Christianized. (It is debatable whether we ever could.) The mission field has shifted to include those who live on your street, in your apartment complex, and at your workplace.

In past generations even the unchurched valued the input and respected the spiritual insight of the church. This is no longer the case. Oprah, Dr. Phil, Deepak Chopra, and other spiritual and relational experts have as much or more influence on how the culture thinks about spiritual matters.

In addition, people view the church as a place where they come once a week to be encouraged so they can go back into the real world and live their real life. And some of the most popular voices on the Christian scene actually agree. While there are millions of people attending these churches, there is a huge segment of our culture that sees the church as irrelevant, and there are plenty of other spiritual options that seem to provide better answers.

There is little we can do about the public image of Western spirituality on a grand scale, but we need to recognize the fact that this is the world at this time. This perspective shapes our next-door neighbors, our office colleagues, and even our family members. And it is so pervasive that simple conversations about these matters will not change anything.

Practice Lessons Part 1

When we see our context for what it is, the need for focus in our Missional Engagement becomes obvious. Our mission field is ripe for God's people to live consistently with one another in a certain way and in a certain place. We no longer need haphazard gospel sharing that is not supported by visible community. We need much more than good sermons, big buildings, and professional video presentations. We need a people committed to *specific places* who are called to bring redemption to those places.

Since I have used the word *neighborhood* to talk about where we are present, it might seem redundant to talk about the need for proximity. In our fast-paced, transient culture, however, we rarely think about how the gospel relates to a location. We primarily envision how it impacts individuals. As a result, words are all we have to offer most people.

But when we think about being called to focus on a specific location, we then can see beyond just the individuals to what is going on in the neighborhoods. How can God's community bring redemption to an elementary school? How would the firemen at a local fire station be impacted by a community that adopted them? What impact might a group have on one group member's workplace if they committed to pray for and even relate to the workers there?

139

The kind of neighborhood that a group adopts to demonstrate God's presence will vary from group to group. For some it might be a few blocks or a street, even if some group members live in a different part of town. For others it might be a school with a high percentage of at-risk children. Some might be called to work with a specific people group. Yet another group might see opportunities to demonstrate God's kingdom in unique ways at the workplace.

The key is proximity, because only with it can things like repetition of contact, regular encounters, inclusion in everyday activities, and the like occur. To be focused on a specific local context will require long-term investment and being present repeatedly.

This is how those called to be missionaries in a foreign country think about ministry. They are not called to the entire world or to the entire country. There is a call to a specific country and usually to a specific group of people within that country. They think about the local situation and the specific people within that local context. If even 10 percent of all the Christian groups in North America took such an approach, the impact would surprise us.

Practice Lessons Part 2

I was tempted to leave this section out because it will offend many of you. But in good conscience, I cannot. After working with churches for nearly two decades, I have seen one consistent problem with people actually doing this practice. Some of the people who have the most to offer neighborhoods are also the busiest at keeping the organization of the church going. All of their volunteer time is spent working in committees, singing in the choir, leading youth events for kids in the church, teaching in Sunday school, and attending up to three services per week. Sometimes it seems like the more committed to God a person becomes, the less he or she is involved with the neighborhood. This seems to be especially true of those who are paid employees of local churches.

To enter into Missional Engagement with the neighborhood is not synonymous with maintaining the organization of the church and all of its trappings. An early small group visionary and former missionary to South America reflects on this by contrasting a kingdom focus with a church focus:

Kingdom people seek first the Kingdom of God and its justice; church people often put the church work above concerns of justice, mercy and truth. Church people think about how to get people into the church; Kingdom people think about how to get the church into the world. Church people worry that the world might change the church; Kingdom people work to see the church change the world.[1]

These are harsh words, but we need to consider them. Those reading this who are participants in house churches, organic groups, or simple churches may not identify with this; however, the more a church develops, the more complex it can become over time and more energy is required to run the organizational side of things.

What should be done? If there ever was a complex question, this is one, and I do not dare give easy answers to it. Church leaders, group leaders, and group members must work together and listen to God about this. If people who feel a sense of urgency to focus on their neighborhood are not released to do so, then missional life will never transpire. The church needs people who are willing to think outside the box and have the time to simply talk with their neighbors and invest their life in them. On what is God calling you to focus?

Use the following space to record your reflections on this practice:

Practice: Speaking Peace

When you enter a house, first say, "Peace to this house."

Luke 10:5

When a group focuses on a specific neighborhood, what then? What does it have to offer the people? In other words, what stance does it take when going out to the neighborhood?

141

A Stance of Power

In many situations groups have related to neighborhoods from the stance of power. The people within the groups have determined that they have special revelation from God that those outside the church need, and their job is to tell them the truth. Because of their knowledge, they have power, and they feel called to *inform* those without this knowledge of their ignorance.

This stance is combative in nature. The goal of ministry to those outside the church is to convince them of the validity of Christianity. Therefore, they work up all the energy and conviction they can to go to war with the ignorance of the *infidels* of the world.

Consider most of the gospel presentation approaches that have been used in the last century. Almost all of them depend upon a unilateral or one-way conversation where the one with the Christian insight tells the one without it what it means to be a Christian. This approach creates little opportunity for dialogue or conversation.

The combative stance results in one of two actions: *fight* or *flight*. Those who *fight* feel compelled to share this gospel message and are usually good at articulating a point and convincing others to see things their way. But most of the church has opted for *flight*. They are worn out by the combative approach, and they find they are never able to win people to Jesus. As a result, they simply withdraw into their Christian enclave because they don't see any other alternative for sharing the gospel with people they know.

Another Way

A combative stance offers only two alternatives for sharing Jesus with others. But this win-lose, right-wrong approach to sharing the message of Jesus does not fit Jesus's message at all. Of course, it would be improper to beat someone until he or she prays to receive Jesus, but it has long been acceptable to *bully* people with words until they accept Jesus as Lord. I wonder how many people have *prayed the prayer* just to get Christians to shut up.

When Jesus sent out the seventy-two disciples to proclaim the kingdom, he told them to enter a home by proclaiming *peace*. This is much more than saying a word. When proclaiming peace, a person actually embodies a stance contrary to a combative one. In the Gospel of Luke, *peace* is used as another way of saying *salvation*. Much more than simply the absence of war or social discord, it calls for a positive or proactive stance represented by the Old Testament word *shalom*, which means communal well-being. In the biblical story, *peace* is a gift of God upon his people to live in security, blessing, and relational wholeness.

When those sent out two by two entered a home, they were to proclaim *peace* with their mouths, thereby offering God's well-being to those people. Not a cheap sales pitch for the kingdom, a mini-sermon to get them to pray a prayer, nor an invitation hung on the door to attend a church service. They came in a stance of peace, offering themselves to the people in the neighborhood.

Practice Lessons

The apostle Paul says that the fruit of the Spirit includes *peace* (see Gal. 5:22). The Spirit of God sends God's people into the neighborhoods with his fruit. Christians can be the embodiment of peace if in fact they are full of the Spirit and peace and wholeness reside within them and through them as they go out with the message of peace. The Spirit of God actually lives within your group members. How can you better listen to the Spirit and be led by the Spirit?

Often, learning to practice peace with our neighbors begins as we respond in peace when group conflict arises. Can group members choose the way of peace rather than the need to win? Choosing the way of peace does not mean ignoring reality or covering things up so that emotions are set aside. Peace actually creates an environment in which each person can offer their perspective and deal with differences because no one feels the pressure to win. Then when people in our neighborhoods see us dealing with conflict in peaceful ways, they will notice the difference and wonder who this God we serve is.

In practicing peace with one another, group members can offer a way of doing life that is not shaped by the combative stance of this world. They learn to enter the neighborhood with dialogue and conversations as opposed to assuming that the Christians inside the group have the answers for those outside the church.

This offer of peace directly confronts the language of growth and multiplication that has shaped the small group landscape.

Group multiplication is often elevated as the primary measurement of effectiveness in sharing the gospel. In many churches, this has created a fixation on numbers. Goal-oriented, type A leaders like tangible goals, and growth in members and group multiplication is the most concrete way to measure what is going on in the group.

The problem is that this focus on numerical goals can turn into a form of violence. Parker Palmer writes, "By violence I mean any way we have of violating the identity and integrity of another person. I find this definition helpful because it reveals the critical connections between violent acts large and small—from dropping bombs on civilians halfway around the world to demeaning a child in a classroom."[2]

This kind of violence (or combative stance) is not limited to the wars fought between countries. In fact it is so common to our everyday life that we don't even recognize that it is there. And it creeps into the church as soon as we objectify those outside the faith and put non-Christians into categories, describe them as target audiences, or make them part of our group's growth goals.

We don't need goals to win people for Jesus or multiply our groups by a certain date. This generates a stance within us that is contrary to the nature of the Good News. It turns what we are doing "in the name of Jesus" into an objective that is not in his name at all. We simply need to establish the goal of being a people who have something to offer that is contrary to what is found in the world. We don't need to win. We don't need to convince. We simply aim to be a people of peace in the midst of cultures that are ruled by violence.

We see this through the tensions, the differences, the challenges, and the questions discovered as we enter the neighborhood. The differences are present—whether in the form of religious pluralism, moral relativism, cultural diversity, or just simple personality differences—and as we engage them, we have the opportunity to enter into conversations about the differences. Rather than going in *with guns ablaze* trying to fix the neighborhood, we ask questions, listen, and enter into dialogue.

One of the greatest ways of offering peace is to ask people to share their stories. Of course, we go with the message of the kingdom and the story of God, but if we want them to hear God's story, we must listen to what is going on in their lives. Then as we listen, we will see where the violence reigns in their lives and then can offer the alternative of peace, wholeness, and the well-being of God.

Use the following space to record your reflections on this practice:

Practice: Observe

So, because Jesus was doing these things on the Sabbath, the Jewish leaders began to persecute him. In his defense Jesus said to them, "My Father is always at his work to this very day, and I too am working." For this reason they tried all the more to kill him; not only was he breaking the Sabbath, but he was even calling God his own Father, making himself equal with God. Jesus gave them this answer: "Very truly I tell you, the Son can do nothing by himself; he can do only what he sees his Father doing, because whatever the Father does the Son also does."

John 5:16–19

What is God already doing in the neighborhood? We must learn to engage people with the assumption that God is already at work in this world and our calling is to discover where he is at work so that we can join him.

We Are Not Saviors

When I reflect on the various ways I have been taught about how to share Jesus with people, there are two basic streams. First, there is the *evangelical* stream, which emphasizes the importance of preaching the gospel of Jesus Christ and leading people to acknowledge Jesus as Lord. The second stream has historically been labeled *social justice*, which emphasizes not words but actions taken by the church to bring justice to those who have been marginalized in society.

In the last few years many writers and preachers have acknowledged that these two streams should flow together instead of being separated as they have been in the past. This is true, but there is a more essential problem that these two streams share: both have been shaped by a basic belief that those in the church have something to offer those outside the church. Those from the evangelical stream are taught that they have a message to offer the lost. Those from the social justice stream are taught that they have a better way of life to offer those who have been marginalized. And while there is some truth in each of these beliefs, both streams place the onus upon those in the church to go out and do something. It is as if the fate of the world and the future of lost souls is absolutely dependent upon Christians going out and doing one of these forms of sharing Jesus.

But we are not the builders of God's kingdom. That is God's job. We are not the savior of someone's soul. God is. We do not bring justice to injustice. God does. This reality is so easy to miss because we are activists by nature. We are shaped by the worldview of "getting things done" to accomplish a goal. If the goal is to reach people for Jesus, there are specific strategies for doing so, and the weight of that falls upon us.

Jesus said that he only did what he saw his Father doing. For goal-oriented activists who like to get things done, this is a hard teaching to embrace. If God is at work in a neighborhood before we enter it, then if we presume we know what is needed, we could actually be working against God instead of with him. We must get over the *savior complex* that pervades the church. We must be willing to admit that we don't have all of the answers; we don't have a fine-tuned message to share; we don't know what the marginalized people in our society need. We must refuse to offer prepackaged, easy answers to difficult questions.

146

Who's Listening?

We must also be willing to admit the fact that no one in the neighborhood is really listening to the church in the first place. They might acknowledge that the church has some good stuff to say about spiritual things, but the church no longer is viewed as having a valid voice in the way we do life. Most think that church, God, and the talk about church and God might mean a lot to insiders, but these things are primarily for those insiders. These are not things that have any real bearing on those outside the *church club*.

We cannot assume then that people care about what God, the church, or the Bible has to say about anything. That is not the language of our society anymore. Even with the creative churches that have arisen and grown to huge numbers in the last decade, most people in our society still don't care what we are doing within the four walls of our buildings. Their lives are full enough. Why would they want to add more?

Nor do they even care how great our small groups are. They are not interested in how good the Bible study is or if we are using some new DVD curriculum. Most people don't want another meeting in their lives, so trying to sell them on the need to attend a group is like trying to sell a new car in a village without roads.

Those within the church use insider language to share Jesus with outsiders, thinking that there is shared understanding and values. But those outside the church see the church quite differently. And because we fail to realize this, our words land on deaf ears.

Practice Lessons

In Luke 10, Jesus instructs his disciples to announce peace, and then he says, "If the head of the house loves peace, your peace will rest on that house; if not, it will return to you" (v. 6). The disciples are to talk peace or salvation to people, but the way they do this is by first observing how people respond to them. They are to discover what God is already doing in and through them and see if the people in that house love salvation. If so, then those in the house will receive God's salvation, but if not, they will reject it.

This requires that we enter neighborhoods as learners. We go to observe, listen, and receive feedback. We do not go with the arrogant presumption that we know what people need. We ask questions. We talk about needs. We listen to their pain.

We learn what is transpiring in individuals' lives. In our world, there are a lot of people who are in pain as a result of encounters with churches. If we are not willing to listen to that pain and let people work through what they feel, then nothing will be gained.

As we listen and observe, we learn about the people who are looking for peace or wholeness. We discover those who are searching, asking questions, or maybe facing struggles that are forcing them to reevaluate life. When we go as learners, we gain credibility for what we eventually say. We simply tap into what God is doing and work with that. We don't need to feel pressured to make something happen, to get people to pray a prayer, or to accomplish some great thing in the name of justice.

We also go to learn what is going on in the community or the neighborhood as a whole. We learn to ask questions about how people perceive the community, such as these:

- What do you think is our community's greatest asset?
- What do you think is our community's greatest need?
- If you could change one thing about our community, what would it be?
- What do you think is the best thing about living or working here?[3]

Research has consistently confirmed that between 80 and 90 percent of any church is comprised of people who were influenced to acknowledge Christ as Lord by a relative, friend, or coworker. Most people are influenced for Jesus by people they trust. Trust does not come because someone claims to have truth or because a group of people want to do something nice for someone in need. Trust is developed in give-and-take relationships. This means that engaging a neighborhood is not about accomplishing the goal of *getting people saved* or *building the kingdom by growing groups*. It is simply about taking the peace of God to people and entering into conversations with them about life that will reveal where peace is needed. As we listen, observe, and learn, we become friends, which means trust has been established.

Use the following space to record your reflections on this practice:

Practice: Hospitality

Offer hospitality to one another without grumbling.

1 Peter 4:9

Hospitality was one of the distinctive practices that marked the early church as unique in the surrounding culture. The Greek word for hospitality is *philoxenia*, which is a combination of two words: *love* and *stranger*. It basically means "the love of strangers." The practice of hospitality reenacts the hospitality of God. It is the creation of space in one's life for the person who is different or unknown. The early churches were known for this practice, and it was one of the primary ways that the church expanded so quickly without formal structures and organizations. The apostle Paul prioritizes hospitality as a basic practice of the church so much that it is one of the marks of qualification for leadership within the church (see 1 Tim. 3:2; Titus 1:8).

Modern Hospitality

For most of us raised in the church, it is hard to imagine how hospitality relates to being missional. It is so simple, so ordinary, so unspectacular. In my church heritage, we saw it as something that the women who could cook offered on Sunday nights during the fellowship time.

149

Hospitality has become simply one of the programs the church plans at specific times. Often we don't see how it can become a normal way for people to do life together. In addition, our lives are just not conducive to hospitality. Our homes are private places, meant to serve as enclaves from the world. Our life rhythms have taught us to separate the private sphere of our homes from the public sphere of ministry to those who need the Good News. Therefore, the things we do at home are private activities meant for the family or the individual, but not for others.

In addition, the way we eat today makes hospitality almost impossible to practice. We eat on the fly, doing carryout or drive-thru so we can get from one appointment to another. Or if we do sit down to eat with others, we often do so at a neutral, impersonal restaurant.

When we fail at hospitality, we fail at sharing the Good News effectively because hospitality puts life into our words and demonstrates to others that we are interested in them as people rather than just as candidates for group or church membership.

People without a Place

One of the most basic questions we ask about life is: Where do I belong? We are wired to have a place where we feel accepted, loved, and connected. Strangers are "people without a place."[4] One writer on the practice of hospitality explains what it means to be without a place: "To be without a place means to be detached from basic, life-supporting institutions—family, work, polity, religious community—and to be without networks of relations that sustain and support human beings."[5]

If there was ever an era in history when people lack a sense of place, it is now. The average person moves every three to four years, which means they are not in one place nearly long enough to attain any sense of belonging. We have formed a society without roots. In addition, this high rate of relocation impacts familial relationships. Some social philosophers have argued that a sense of belonging partially depends upon close relationships with three generations. But today, even if grandparents live in the same town or city, the parents and kids are often so busy that there is little time for the three generations to interact with each other. Then when you add divorce to the equation, the experience of lacking a place to belong is unavoidable.

Jesus in the Stranger's Face

In one of Jesus's teachings he implies that acts of hospitality are acts of ministry to him. He says,

> When the Son of Man comes in his glory, and all the angels with him, he will sit on his glorious throne. All the nations will be gathered before him, and he will separate the people one from another as a shepherd separates the sheep from the goats. He will put the sheep on his right and the goats on his left.
>
> Then the King will say to those on his right, "Come, you who are blessed by my Father; take your inheritance, the kingdom prepared for you since the creation of the world. For I was hungry and you gave me something to eat, I was thirsty and you gave me something to drink, I was a stranger and you invited me in, I needed clothes and you clothed me, I was sick and you looked after me, I was in prison and you came to visit me."
>
> Then the righteous will answer him, "Lord, when did we see you hungry and feed you, or thirsty and give you something to drink? When did we see you a stranger and invite you in, or needing clothes and clothe you? When did we see you sick or in prison and go to visit you?"
>
> Matthew 25:31–39

Christ comes to the community through the guest, the outsider, the stranger. In this passage, neither those who demonstrated hospitality nor those who failed to do so realized that Christ was coming to them through the stranger. Jesus came in unexpected ways. And because it is unexpected, the invitation to practice hospitality will almost always be inconvenient.

Practice Lessons

There are three concrete aspects of hospitality that make it what it is. First, it is something another experiences in our home. When we open our homes, we create an atmosphere of welcome and conversation. In today's society, this might prove too big a step; therefore you might begin with intermediate places like a coffee shop, a restaurant, or a health club. In Luke 10 the disciples were sent into communities and told to enter homes and receive others' hospitality. Both then and now, the point is the personal nature of the home where the divide between the private and the public is torn down.

The second important aspect of hospitality is food. Hospitality reveals an essential and rudimentary connection between how we eat and how we connect spiritually. The simple physical act of eating has direct impact upon our spirituality and our experience of God. In the Scriptures we are told repeatedly that God entered into the normalcy of life on earth through the incarnation. Take fifteen minutes and skim the book of Luke and count how many times Jesus shared a meal with others.

One of the best ways to learn to share a meal with neighbors is to begin by sharing a regular meal with others in your group. When group members eat together, they are being equipped through this very normal act to open their homes and share meals with those in their neighborhoods.

Third, when offering hospitality, refrain from trying to convert or change the person. By definition, hospitality is a practice that receives people where they are. People in our neighborhoods are not objects to be won. They are people loved by God. The art of hospitality allows others to enter our hearts without expectations. Henri Nouwen states, "Honest receptivity means inviting the stranger into our world on his or her terms, not on ours. When we say, 'You can be my guest if you believe what I believe, think the way I think and behave as I do,' we offer love under a condition or for a price. This leads easily to exploitation, making hospitality into a business."[6]

To embrace a stranger, the one who must take the first step is the host. The host is the one who must change, who must go out and draw in the stranger. Therefore, the only way hospitality works as a practice of Missional Engagement is if the group members change, opening their hearts to receive the stranger as he or she is.

Receptivity, though, is only one side of the coin of hospitality. Receiving the stranger does not mean a group should abdicate what it believes, becoming neutral because of the fear of offending. In true hospitality, the host enters into dialogue with the stranger. Again,

Nouwen steers us correctly: "When we want to be really hospitable we not only have to receive the strangers but also to confront them by an unambiguous presence, not hiding ourselves behind neutrality but showing our ideas, opinions and life style clearly and distinctly."[7]

To begin embracing the stranger is quite simple. Groups only need to make a list of people whom members know in the neighborhood so they can pray for them on a weekly basis. The list need not be long; two people per member is sufficient. From there, the group can host a Matthew Party, named after Matthew the tax collector.[8] He was one of the sinners and tax collectors with whom Jesus related at parties—people who were the rejects of first-century Jewish society (see Matt. 9:9–13). Group members' birthdays provide a good excuse for Matthew Parties. The group can throw a party and invite unchurched friends, family members, neighbors, and coworkers to celebrate the birthday with them.

On a simplified and less organized level, group members can use the power of a shared meal or meeting for coffee to embrace the stranger. The entire small group need not be involved—possibly only a couple or a member from the group. For more guidance on the topic of hospitality, visit www.roxburghmissionalnet.com to download a thirteen-week group discussion and activity guide.

Use the following space to record your reflections on this practice:

Practice: Righting Wrongs

Then Jesus said to his host, "When you give a luncheon or dinner, do not invite your friends, your brothers or sisters, your relatives, or your rich neighbors; if you do, they may invite you back and so you will be repaid. But when you give a banquet, invite the poor, the crippled, the lame, the blind, and you will be blessed. Although they cannot repay you, you will be repaid at the resurrection of the righteous."

Luke 14:12–14

When a group begins to engage a specific neighborhood with the gospel, they will start to recognize patterns of injustice. Some are treated unjustly, others practice injustice, and others idly watch the injustice transpire. The gospel of Jesus Christ is much larger, grander, and proactive than simply sharing a message of *getting saved* so people can go to heaven when they die. Jesus began his ministry by proclaiming the mission on earth and how that relates to the gospel, the Good News:

> The Spirit of the Lord is on me,
> because he has anointed me
> to proclaim good news to the poor.
> He has sent me to proclaim freedom for the prisoners
> and recovery of sight for the blind,
> to set the oppressed free,
> to proclaim the year of the Lord's favor.

Luke 4:18–19

Joining Jesus in his mission of sharing the Good News has huge implications for how we do life while on earth now, not just the state of our soul after death. It relates to the ignored, the marginalized, the outcasts in our neighborhoods. When we see what God is doing in a specific location, we find widows, those entrapped by generational poverty, the physically impaired, and the mentally ill whom he wants us to reach with his love. As I write this chapter, the unemployment rate in this country is over 10 percent. Today there is a new group of the marginalized: the formerly successful people who have lost their jobs.

Encountering Injustice

The nature of injustice in neighborhoods varies from one place to the next. It is easy to make this about *poor* neighborhoods and *rich* neighborhoods, proclaiming that *justice* is about those classified as rich doing something nice for those classified as poor. As a result, justice becomes about *being good deed doers*. With this mind-set, groups might think they are following Jesus in righting wrongs by attending the church's monthly outreach night or doing a periodic service project for the community. But facing injustice is not something we can check off our monthly to-do list so that we can feel proud of our good deeds.

Treating people as a project reinforces the injustice. Instead, we are called to engage people relationally to discover who they are as people. Jesus instructs his people to face injustice personally and to do so by treating those in need as equals.

As we are present in neighborhoods, we will get firsthand knowledge of local injustice. And bringing justice cannot be categorized as simply doing something good for certain people who live in certain *poor* places in the city. Injustice is everywhere, but for the most part we are inoculated to it, often because we are so overwhelmed by what we see, read, and hear in the news that we feel powerless to address it. There is just too much to deal with at that level. But when we encounter it at the local level as it is played out in local people's lives, we can seek God about how we can bring Good News to that local situation.

Practice Lessons

The passage from Luke 14 quoted above highlights the nature of the injustice faced in our neighborhoods. Jesus tells this parable while sitting at dinner with ten to twelve men who are prominent in their village. To his host, an eminent Pharisee, Jesus offers a different way of doing normal life in the village. Instead of inviting those who can repay him with a meal or a party at their home, he should practice inviting those who cannot repay him at all.

With these words, Jesus takes a stand against one of the primary roots of injustice: how we rank people and categorize them into groups. In every society there are the rich, the not as rich, and then those who are marginalized. Typically, like eat with like, which is not much different from how middle school students sit at lunchtime. Jesus attacks this system of excluding those who cannot repay and marginalizing those who are without power.

In Jesus's situation, he speaks to men who live in a small village. They know by name the poor, the crippled, the lame, and the blind of their village. They are not anonymous, nameless masses from the other side of town. They are people these men pass on a daily basis, and by their actions of exclusion the men are performing injustice.

Today we unknowingly reinforce this same pattern of injustice because we naturally connect with people like ourselves; we have relational preferences. Jesus is not challenging the normal pattern of having friends and developing close relationships with people with whom we naturally connect. Jesus is confronting the tyranny of the normal that leads to exclusion.[9]

In group life this tyranny of the normal results in homogeneous groups in which those who gather each week are all part of the same social class or age group. For a long time the church has done couples groups, singles groups, interest groups, and so on. We even create groups for disabled people and the poor. When we begin to engage neighborhoods, we soon discover that not everyone is the same, that *normal* is a combination of people from all these categories.

One of the initial ways we practice Missional Engagement by righting wrongs is *choosing to not choose* who is in our groups. We simply embrace those we engage in our neighborhoods, and as they desire to participate in the life of the group, they become a part. The diversity of the group actually becomes a microcosm of the justice that is sought in the wider community.

What Does God Want to Do?

Yet there is much more to this. Righting wrongs extends beyond having a group of individuals from various backgrounds and ages. In every neighborhood there is a ranking system that creates categories of insiders and outsiders. Jesus identifies them as the poor, the crippled, the lame, and the blind. Those on the margins are unseen and ignored in our culture. In some neighborhoods, the injustice is pervasive. The poverty, racism, maltreatment of the marginalized, and other cruelties are readily visible. In other neighborhoods the injustices and their impact on life lie below the surface. There are the battered wives, abused children, victims of racial profiling, latchkey children, and other less obvious victims of injustice that only become known through relationships.

The missional question for every neighborhood is: What does God want to do? It is impossible to answer this question from the centralized perspective of pastors and church leaders who sit in the church office and organize programs for *reaching the community*. What God wants to do in a neighborhood only becomes clear as a group of people engages the people of that neighborhood and see the needs. As the needs become clear, then a small group can determine if they can address the need or if it requires the involvement of a network of groups working together.

Whatever the need, most likely it will require a spirit of generosity on the part of the group. Generosity comes in all kinds of forms—money being only one. In almost every situation, a group will be challenged to be generous with time. If we are going to fight the *project mentality* in which we treat outsiders as people we do something for, then we must realize that it takes time to be a blessing with our lives. And in doing so, we in turn will be blessed. Bearing God's peace involves the removal of the ranking system that has shaped our world. This requires that those who are marginalized—the mentally handicapped, the former convict, the first-generation immigrant, and so forth—be embraced and included in relational connections.

And by this inclusion, those who are considered *insiders* will be blessed. Jesus meets us through marginalized and needy persons more than we can ever know. We as group members might think we are doing something for others, but in the end, we are the ones most blessed.

Use the following space to record your reflections on this practice:

Practice: Speaking the Gospel

How, then, can they call on the one they have not believed in? And how can they believe in the one of whom they have not heard? And how can they hear without someone preaching to them? And how can anyone preach unless they are sent? As it is written: "How beautiful are the feet of those who bring good news!"

Romans 10:14–15

When I hear a new song on the radio, I never actually hear the words until I have listened to it about five times. But I know if I like a song when I hear it the first time because I know whether or not I like the rhythm.

The same is true of Missional Engagement. The way we live in the neighborhood is what gives us the right to talk about the gospel. The words of the gospel must work in unison with the rhythms of the gospel.

Appropriate Conversations

Christ manifested love by coming to earth. He meets us where we are. When we think about talking of Jesus and salvation to those in our neighborhoods, usually there is only one kind of conversation that comes to mind: some kind of explanation of what it means to be saved. But such a conversation is not appropriate with everyone. To meet them with Christ's love, we must listen to them; we must meet them where they are. James Engel developed the *Engel Scale of Conversion Stages*. Conversion to Christ does not occur through one conversation or one decision. It is a process that transpires over time. It is a journey that people take from being unaware to the point of receiving Christ. The following illustrates the steps of this journey:

−8 Awareness of a Supreme Being but No Effective Knowledge of the Gospel
−7 Initial Awareness of the Gospel
−6 Awareness of the Fundamentals of the Gospel
−5 Grasp of the Implications of the Gospel
−4 Positive Attitude toward the Gospel

158

−3 Personal Problem Recognition
−2 Decision to Act
−1 Repentance and Faith in Christ
  0 The Person Becomes a New Creation in Christ
+1 Post-Decision Evaluation
+2 Incorporation into the Local Church Body
+3 Conceptual and Behavioral Growth[10]

Most evangelism programs assume that everyone is in the same place. They explain how to share Christ with someone who is ready to make a decision to receive Christ (i.e., −1 on the Engel Scale). Our talk about salvation must go to where people are and help them take steps toward Christ rather than assuming they are just unrepentant or hard-hearted because they have not received Christ or attended a church meeting.

In his book *Making Friends for Christ*, Wayne McDill writes, "Evangelism will be effective . . . in direct proportion to its dependence on the establishment and cultivation of meaningful relationships."[11] Part of developing meaningful relationships is understanding how to talk with people, even about things where there may be disagreement. Having appropriate conversations about Jesus and salvation does not mean we avoid the topic because the person is not ready to hear the *plan of salvation*. It means we talk about Jesus in ways that do not require the person to make a decision before he or she has a good understanding of what that means.

Small group meetings can be an effective venue for *seekers* (-4 to -1 on the Engel Scale) to have some of these conversations. But those who have a strong resistance to Jesus might not find a small group meeting a positive experience. Groups are not the preferred medium to awaken people to the reality of God or the message of the gospel. Taking Christ's love to people requires creativity, friendship, prayer, and time—all of which can be done outside of meetings.

Practice Lessons Part 1

Recently I read the book of Acts straight through, as I would if I were reading a short story. I noticed something I had never seen

159

before. Luke records many different ways the disciples spoke of Jesus, the gospel, and salvation. They basically told the story of Jesus: how he was sent by God to be the Messiah, was rejected, died on the cross for their sin, and rose from the grave. This was followed by an invitation to repent, that is, realign their thinking and life around this Jesus. (See Acts 3:11–26 as an example of this.)

This is a helpful way of thinking about our conversations about Jesus in the neighborhoods. Actually, for many Christians it is a reconceiving because they have been taught to lay out principles regarding sin, the need for a Savior, and repentance. The gospel as shared by the first Christians was not first a list of principles that must be believed in order to become a Christ follower. It was first a story—one about their encounter with Jesus. The Good News of the gospel is about this Jesus who came, died, and rose again so that we might have life and the kingdom of God might expand on the earth.

Later in Acts, Luke records similar conversations initiated by the apostle Paul. He tells the same story about Jesus, but Paul does so differently. He uses his personal encounter with the risen Christ on the road to Damascus as the entry point. Paul tells how he lived one way and the beliefs he had about Jesus while living that way. Then he explains what happened when he was smitten blind, heard the voice of Jesus, and then was healed of the blindness. This is followed by an explanation of how Paul's life had changed since then.

Paul basically shared the Good News of Jesus through his personal testimony. He did not depend upon theological abstraction or in-depth apologetics to initiate the conversation. Such conversations may have been appropriate at other points, but no one can argue with the experience of a changed life. Often all that is required is simply saying, "I once lived this way, I encountered Jesus, and now my life is different, and here is how . . ."

When we do this, two things occur: First, we are doing what friends do—sharing our stories. Even if someone is a -8 on the Engel Scale, it is still appropriate to share who we are and what Jesus means, even though they have a totally different perspective. Second, by sharing our story of Jesus, we are opening the door to conversation and dialogue as opposed to simply telling people what to think about Jesus.

As questions and objections arise, then those can be addressed in a variety of ways, including the use of outside resources like books or other people.

Practice Lessons Part 2

As we listen to our neighbors and share our stories, they will begin to share their own stories more freely. We will hear about how they do life, what they like to do, and what they don't. We will also hear about the challenges they face in life that might present ways we can demonstrate how the Good News of Jesus can meet them where they are. I remember the first time a friend asked me about my relationship with Jesus and how he might help with depression. I was shocked that I did not have to force my story; rather, it came up in natural conversation. When people face issues such as those in the following list, they are often open to conversations that might cause them to think about God in a new and different way:

- Marriage, divorce, separation
- Pregnancy or the birth of a child
- Death of a spouse, child, or family member
- A layoff from work or an employment change
- A marital reconciliation in process
- Help needed in child rearing
- Change in work responsibilities
- Foreclosure or financial struggles
- Sexual difficulties or need for marriage enrichment

When people hear our stories and listen to the rhythms of our lives, they will see that salvation is much more than a personal choice related to life after death or a private decision about personal beliefs. They see how the Good News actually changes the way we live. It gives them access to not only the God who can change their lives but also a community that can embrace them and walk with them through their life situations. Jesus called this the kingdom of God. As we share the gospel, we are inviting people to take steps toward Jesus and his way in the kingdom. In fact, this is what the missional community is doing for each other even though they are already saved. They are challenging each other to walk and work out their salvation each day. This is the journey of missional community.

Use the following space to record your reflections on this practice:

9

Being Formed to
Lead Missional Group Life

During the last year, many church leaders have asked me how they can train their leaders differently in order to help them effectively lead missional small groups. In some ways my response would call for an additional book to adequately address this topic, but in other ways the response is so simple that we can easily miss the point. We miss it because we often look for leadership training that focuses on skills development. The questions asked in such training always focuses on the *how* question. The reality, however, is that leading a missional group is more about the *who* question. I have written this book as an invitation to be and live differently. Being missional will not result from a list of how-tos we can follow; developing the skills to lead a missional group will not occur when a person simply abandons one set of leadership techniques and adopts another.

Leading missional groups occurs as leaders are formed and shaped for mission. We have to think and lead differently when the purpose of the group moves from simply getting churched people to attend groups to moving our experience of community back into the neighborhoods. And this is especially true when we realize that those in our neighborhoods are not that interested in coming to church as it has traditionally been conceived. Over the last couple of years, I have been helping pastors understand what it means to be a missional leader using the concepts developed by my colleagues Alan Roxburgh and Fred Romanuk, in the book *The Missional Leader*.[1] In it they identify four categories or areas of leadership skills that leaders must develop when they begin leading others on mission. While their book applies these four categories to the broader role of leading the organization we traditionally call the church, the principles apply to leading missional groups as well.

The four categories or areas include:

1. The Character of a Missional Leader
2. Skills for Cultivating People for Mission
3. Skills for Forming a Missional Environment
4. Imaginative Ability to Engage the Context

When we think about leadership through these four areas, we discover key elements of group leadership that have often been overlooked in many of the group leader training programs that are currently being used.

Area #1: Character

First, we must recognize that leadership of this sort flows out of who the leader is as much or more than what he or she does. In fact, according to Roxburgh and Romanuk, the other three areas of leadership flow out of and are dependent on this one. All four areas influence one another, but this one is foundational. They illustrate it in this way:

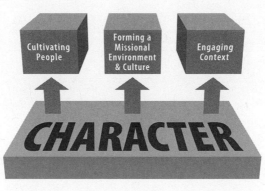

When I first started leading a group, I did not think much about my personal leadership attributes: maturity, trust, and integrity. The focus was primarily on things like how to lead a group meeting, the purpose of the groups, and how to pastor people. I guess the character of the leader was always assumed and that we only needed to discuss the technical aspects of leading groups.

Sometimes, people assume that personal leadership attributes depend on the length someone has been a Christian or how old someone is. Research has repeatedly proven that this is not the case. Young Christians have proven to lead effectively out of a foundation of character just as much as established Christians.[2] Age or how long someone has been a Christian are not the telling factors. There are other things God is developing in us to make us leaders of character.

In her book *Call to Commitment*, Elizabeth O'Connor chronicles the story of Church of the Savior in Washington DC, which was one of the first churches in the last century to experiment with mission groups. She writes about the key points the pastor, Gordon Cosby, taught to their leaders. In all of my reading on small group leadership, this piece stands out as unique—so much so that I found it necessary to quote some of what they taught because it arises out of rich experience and the book is no longer in print. She discusses six qualities of leadership, all of which relate to the foundation of character.[3]

1. Knowledge That Comes from Self-Reflection

"First," Gordon says, "a person must come to that place where he knows that the real issue is always an internal one." This is a difficult lesson to learn. The temptation of the natural man is to focus on what is wrong "out there." Leaders want to blame circumstances and other people for struggles and failures, but it is crucial that leaders begin with the only person they have the authority to change or control: themselves.

2. Capacity to Take Hostility

Gordon taught his leaders that hostility would be a normal part of leading missional community. In fact, he prepared his leaders to understand that if a group was going to have any depth to it and therefore anything to give a hurting world, that hostility would be part of the process. O'Connor writes:

> The second quality of leadership is the capacity to take hostility. The mission group especially is hit by this not only from without but from within its life. . . . The mission group does not produce hostility in its members. We bring it with us into the group and there, for many reasons, it is uncovered.

Missional life will require people to invest their whole selves, not just the parts they want others to see. In most of our relationships, we keep hidden problems, emotions, and struggles. We present ourselves as a little better than we are. This tendency won't go away in a missional small group experience, but the conflicts will arise more frequently. And leaders must expect this fact and be willing to walk through the hostility.

3. Capacity to Accept Others

Gordon understood that we cannot work with people where we want them to be, but we have to relate to them where they actually are. Too often leaders put pressure on those they lead to be other than where they are currently located on their journey with Christ. This only produces artificial growth. O'Connor explains:

> A third closely related quality is the capacity to accept another person where he is. There is a bit of the manipulator in all of us and a bit of the perfectionist. We tend to set standards for ourselves and standards for others, and to become critical if they are not met.

Such standards or ideals can actually kill the life of a group. The expectations that the group will operate a certain way and accomplish pre-set goals can generate criticism and bitterness. God actually works with where people are not with where the leaders might want them to be. And the reality is that most of us are not nearly close to any kind of ideal that others set for us. But when leaders release the members to engage reality, the group will experience a freedom to move forward and walk in the mission.

4. *Ability to Prioritize Significant Issues*

The needs discovered as we go on mission are much bigger than any one group or even group of groups can meet. Needs will always be there, and one of the best ways to get off mission is to fail to understand where our priorities should lie. Here is how they talked about it at Church of the Savior:

> A fourth quality of leadership is the perspective which enables us to sort the little issues from the big ones. Sometimes we expand the little issues out of all proportion, thinking that in so doing we are maintaining our individuality and integrity as persons.

Leaders are called to help people gain focus and listen to what God has called them to do. This does not occur by fiat but through conversations where varying points of view are processed. Through such conversations, the group can process the specific nature of its mission, remind each other of their calling, and set realistic boundaries.

5. *Willingness to Fail*

Mission will require risk, and no one takes risks without the possibility of failure. This is one of the reasons I often encourage churches to start off with missional small groups by calling them experiments. Failure is a good teacher, and if you understand that the journey into mission is about "failing forward"—an attitude of learning from mistakes while moving on—then you will have the freedom to learn along the way. O'Connor reveals:

> The fifth quality of leadership is a willingness to fail and to let others fail. . . . Behind this is the conviction that if God does a new thing through us, we must necessarily be trying that which has not been tried before and there will be no way of knowing in advance the outcome.

New experiments will mean that some people will try things that just won't work. It will also mean that some of them will simply be off track. However, with every experiment, groups will learn. They will discover new ways of engaging their neighbors. Without such experiments groups would only be stuck in what they already know.

6. *Genuine Care for People*

This one point is the most important. And believe it or not, it cannot be attained by reading books on group leadership or attending the best training in the world. God is forming his leader from the inside out with his character of love. He desires to teach us to love others as he loves.

> The sixth quality which Gordon gives sounds deceptively simple. . . . Gordon sums it up, "Our mission is to be able to say convincingly to another person, 'I love you, and I always will.'"

Without love, all the good works a group can do are only empty actions. Without love, the deepest needs within people will be missed and eventually groups will grow weak in their efforts. Leaders must seek God for a real care and concern for the people in the group and for those with whom the group shares God's love. Without this, we lack the most basic element of being missional.

Area #2: Cultivating People

While this book has not directly spoken to specific ways of leading a missional small group, through and through, it has been a book about just that. It just speaks about it in a different way. It serves as a basic music book for missional rhythms to help you get started on the journey of living and being a person who embodies missional community. The rhythms provided demonstrate practical ways to move forward in missional life, and thereby they show leaders ways to cultivate people on this journey.

You could dive into practicing them, and I encourage you to do so, but even better, talk with a few people who you think might be open to practicing these with you. The best way to lead a missional small group is to do it with a team. In fact, one of the differences between leading a normal small group and leading a missional group is that you learn to lead as a part of a team who hears God together. These people might be part of your existing group, or they might be friends whom you believe are open to forming an experimental group that will test out these concepts and see what works. Elizabeth O'Connor makes a similar point when talking about love and caring for people: "Unless there are two or three persons with the capacity to love at the heart of a mission group, it is doomed."[4]

Try to work as a team in your leadership. Have the humility to admit that you cannot do it alone. In fact, you don't have to do it alone. Find two or three people who want to cultivate people together.

As you go forward, seek out the counsel and input of a leader who can help you on the journey. Talk with your pastor or other church leader about what you are doing. Even if he or she doesn't have much experience in this kind of venture, ask someone to pray with you and spend some time talking with you about what you are doing. You can also partner with other groups that are on the same journey and learn from each other as you go.

Area #3: Forming a Missional Environment

Every leader must learn and develop the basic skills required to facilitate a meeting, ask good questions, guide the group in mutual ministry and prayer time, and administrate the various parts of group life. A leader must be aware of basic dos and don'ts that are essential to how effective groups work. Over the last fifty years we have learned a lot about small group dynamics from both inside and outside the church.

For instance, when starting a group meeting, people need some kind of warm-up activity or discussion before diving into worship or Bible discussion. Often these are called icebreakers. Some groups do this with food, others are adept at casual conversation, and others use an icebreaker question to help people open up. Learning how to ask good icebreakers and get conversation going can really help a leader.

There are many good training courses, books, web-based magazines, and blogs that address these issues. I encourage leaders to read one book per year on group leadership, even if they have gone through the official church training or have lots of group leading experience. See appendix B for a list of resources on this topic.

Even though missional small groups are different from normal small groups, there are some universal principles that apply to almost every small group. Most of the key leadership and group dynamics principles can be applied to all four stories. Here is a list of basic topics that you will find in the best resources on small group dynamics:

- How to open meetings
- How to effectively host a group
- How to lead a group in worship
- How to facilitate conversations in group discussion
- How to ask good questions
- How to create a welcoming environment
- How to include new people in the group
- How to minister to difficult people—for example, the talker, the blamer, the avoider, the know-it-all
- How to lead people into deeper levels of communication

When a group shifts into a missional mind-set of group life, there is one specific thing in which most groups need good leadership: the way they talk. When we do Christian-focused normal groups over an extended period, we develop insider language, Bible speak, that can create an us/them mentality. Members say things like "the righteousness of God," use Greek words like *agape* or *phileo*, repeat popular phrases of their pastor, and make quick Bible references. Or they tell insider jokes that only those with a long history with the group or church would know. I don't think that most do this in a way that is meant to be exclusive. It is just simply common to develop a shared language for those who "belong" to a group.

A crucial skill for leaders is that of helping a group talk in such a way that outsiders feel as though they can actually share in the conversation. In other words, all of the "how-to" topics listed above can be led very well using insider language, but when we start engaging people who don't know our language or even care to know it, we must learn to talk about God, the gospel, and Jesus in a way that does not require them to learn a new vocabulary.

Area #4: Engaging the Context

At this point in history, God is forming his people to be missionaries in our own land. He is shaping us to be a people with a greater need to love than to be loved. As we become this people of love, a people who play the rhythms of God's life, we become a sign to the world of what true life is really about. We become outposts of light in the midst of the darkness. Down our streets, in our subdivisions, in the inner-city, at the workplace, in our schools, we become players of God's music.

This requires us to listen to what is going on in the lives of our group members. We cannot assume that a one-size-fits-all kind of group will work in every situation. Shift workers might meet in the middle of the night, executives over lunch, or youth at the school building. We need to learn to listen to the realities of our lives and see how God wants to meet us there.

A few years ago a youth pastor told me this story. A sixteen-year-old daughter of a gang leader had given her life to Jesus. Her father forbade her from attending anything that looked like an official church meeting. Little did he know that there was a small group of students who met at her school, led by other students. This group supported her, shared the Bible with her, and prayed for her. She got infected with the love of God so much that she visited her former boyfriend who had treated her abusively and was now in prison on death row. She shared the Good News of Jesus with him and he gave his life to Christ. He in turn was able to lead twenty-six other inmates to give their lives to Christ. This one girl's life was changed and then twenty-seven other lives were changed because a group of people decided to live differently in order to have an impact on the world.

Instead of forcing this group that met at the school into normal church patterns, the leaders simply worked with what God was already doing in their neighborhood. Likewise, we need not assume that he is absent or that people are not already asking questions. We need to go with listening ears ready to learn about their lives, not just trying to get them to come to our groups. We should have the most to offer these people, and this means creating space in our lives to simply listen.

It also requires us to ask what God wants to do in our neighborhoods. How does God want to use you and your group? What gifts and passions do you have that he can redeem? Where are the ignored people? Where are the outcasts? And how do your gifts and those needs match up?

A pastor in North Texas tells of a story of a faithful member who was also a hockey coach. The problem was that the games in the boys' league that he coached were almost always played on Sunday mornings. He came to the church leadership and explained how he was committed to the church but also felt called to coach. From this arose an idea to start a chapel-like experience for families involved with the team. By no means was it mandatory, but neither was it simply an alternative church service for churched people. People came who didn't previously go to church, and a few entrusted their lives to Christ for the first time.[5]

As we go forward, it will require that we experiment and learn along the way. This is the way we learn to play an instrument. We don't suddenly know how to play a guitar unless we actually start playing. Your experiments with playing missional music will be far from perfect. But that is not the reason we do it. We do it simply because this is what Jesus is up to in our world. Recently, our church did a ten-week series on ministering to those entrapped by poverty in our church. As I was developing some of the curriculum, I became overwhelmed by the vast need I was seeing. While reflecting on how I was feeling, I sensed this impression: God is already bringing the Good News of salvation to those in need, even though I don't see it. Then it hit me: I have the opportunity to get involved with what Jesus is already doing. I can ignore this invitation and miss out on Jesus or I can venture out with him and play some new music.

Appendix A

Getting Started with a Missional Experiment

Following is a thirteen-step process to help a group experiment and learn how to be missional along the way. This is not a list of ideas but a way for your group to reflect on and discuss what you hear God saying about the call of the group. This process depends upon the group listening to the Spirit of God and to the Scriptures. In other words, it is not a process of simply going out and doing something called *missional*.

Different groups will learn missional rhythms at different speeds. Some will pick them up quickly, while others will develop them slowly. Speed is not the key to effectiveness; consistency is. Even the most gifted and creative musicians practice the basics repeatedly. One studio guitarist was asked how he plays with such excellence. He responded, "Every day I repeatedly practice the basic chords that a novice learns." The goal of the steps below is to help a group learn the basics and then introduce and practice them consistently.

These steps work best if the group takes twelve to fifteen weeks to go through the first twelve steps. Then in step thirteen the group will determine next steps regarding what it needs to process further. For most groups, it will take intentional focus over a period of six months to a year in order for these rhythms to become second nature.

The short teaching segments can be downloaded as video files that can be viewed at www.roxburghmissionalnet.com.

Step 1: Introduce the Idea of Missional Small Groups

Opening Question: If you were a historian in the year 2200 and were given the task of understanding everyday life of the average North American in the decade beginning in 2010, what words would you use? (Allow ten minutes.)

Short Teaching: How Group Life Can Change This

Take ten to fifteen minutes to explain the four stories of group life. Emphasize how the first two basically assume the normal life of North America and place a meeting on top and how the last two are about the creation of a group that lives differently than the normal life.

Note: If group members have the opportunity to read chapters one through four, they will be able to contribute to this teaching time.

Discussion Questions

Allow twenty to thirty minutes for the people to process the four stories through discussing these questions:

1. How has our group been a normal group that is simply an addition to our normal lives?
2. In what ways has this normal group experience been beneficial?
3. In what ways have you longed for more from the group experience?
4. How can a group help people live in a way that is different from the normal life experience?

174

Step 2: Introduce the Three Rhythms

Opening Question: What are the normal activities of our group? (Write responses on a large piece of paper.)

Short Teaching: The Rhythms of Missional Community

During this time, introduce how missional small groups are distinct by how they practice the rhythms of Missional Communion, Missional Relating, and Missional Engagement. Then conclude by passing out a copy of the twenty-one missional practices, which can be downloaded from www.roxburghmissionalnet.com. This teaching corresponds with chapter 5.

Discussion Questions

1. What stands out to you from this teaching?
2. How does the way we relate to God impact how we are on mission?
3. How do our relationships with each other impact how we are on mission?
4. How might adopting a few of these practices change our lives?
5. How might it change our group?

Step 3: Pick Three Rhythms

Opening Question: What is your favorite kind of music? Why?

Short Teaching: Learning to Play Music

If someone in your group has had some kind of music lessons, ask that person to share how he or she began to learn to play that instrument. When learning a new instrument, you begin with very simple lessons that help to create a basic knowledge of how the instrument works.

This teaching focuses on how to begin and learn some basic rhythms without trying to do all twenty-one practices at once, which would be like trying to swallow a watermelon whole. The rest of the teaching focuses on the various elements required to effectively learn a new instrument: desire to learn, time to practice, the basic instructions about how to play, and a music teacher.

Discussion Questions

1. Of the twenty-one practices on the list, are there any that we as a group do relatively well? (For questions 2, 3, and 4, make a list on a large piece of paper to see where individual group members' interests lie.)
2. Of the seven listed under Missional Communion, which two interest you the most?
3. Of the seven listed under Missional Relating, which two interest you the most?
4. Of the seven listed under Missional Engagement, which two interest you the most?
5. As a group, pick one from each of the three rhythms to begin practicing.

Step 4: Missional Communion Practice—Introduction

Opening Question: What is one thing you see God changing in your life?

Short Teaching: Introduction to the First of the Three Practices Chosen (from the Twenty-one Listed) by the Group

Provide a basic overview of the practice chosen for Missional Communion.

Discussion Questions

1. How might this practice change our group? Our individual lives?
2. In what ways might this practice help us have an impact upon the world around us?
3. What information about this practice would be helpful?
4. What is one way that we could practice this during the next week?

Step 5: Missional Communion Practice—Hindrances

Opening Question: How have you seen God in the normal stuff of life over the last week?

Short Teaching: Life Hindrances

This teaching focuses on how the normal stuff of life is what hinders how we practice our faith. We need to avoid guilt and manipulation to try to make people line up with the practices. Instead we need to talk about how we normally do life and see how that impacts how we follow Jesus. The basic content of this teaching is taken from chapter 2.

Discussion Questions

1. How successful were you in putting the agreed-upon practice from last week into action?
2. How did you feel when you succeeded? Failed?
3. What were some of the things in your life that hindered you from practicing it?
4. What kind of support or encouragement from the group would help you address some of these hindrances?

Step 6: Missional Communion Practice—Habits

Opening Question: What do you see God doing in your life to change you?

Short Teaching: Forming New Habits

This teaching will help the group see that missional community is about a journey, not a destination. God is working through the group and in individuals to bring about this life by empowering them to develop new habits. The content of this chapter is roughly based on that found in chapter 4.

Discussion Questions

1. What are some habits that you do without thinking?

2. What has been the biggest challenge related to doing the chosen practice?
3. How is God using this practice to change your life?
4. What is something you can do to help make this practice a habit?

Step 7: Missional Relating Practice—Introduction

Apply the process from step 4 to the Missional Relating Practice you have chosen.

Step 8: Missional Relating Practice—Hindrances

Apply the process from step 5 to the Missional Relating Practice you have chosen.

Step 9: Missional Relating Practice—Habits

Apply the process from step 6 to the Missional Relating Practice you have chosen.

Step 10: Missional Engagement Practice

Apply the process from step 4 to the Missional Engagement Practice you have chosen.

Step 11: Missional Engagement Practice

Apply the process from step 5 to the Missional Engagement Practice you have chosen.

Step 12: Missional Engagement Practice

Apply the process from step 6 to the Missional Engagement Practice you have chosen.

Step 13: What's Next?

Opening Question: How has our group changed since we began this process?

Discussion Questions

1. What impact have we had upon our neighbors in this process?
2. How has this process been different than you expected?
3. What has been the biggest challenge?
4. What has been the most rewarding?
5. How can we continue developing these practices into habits?
6. What's next for our group?

Appendix B

Key Resources for Missional Small Groups

Books on the Missional Church

Foolishness to the Greeks, by Lesslie Newbigin

Introducing the Missional Church: What It Is, Why It Matters and How to Become One, by Alan J. Roxburgh and M. Scott Boren

The Missional Leader, by Alan Roxburgh and Fred Romanuk

The Relational Way: From Small Group Structures to Holistic Life Connections, by M. Scott Boren. (While this book is not directly about the missional church, it does identify the crucial structural issues required within a church to promote missional small groups.)

Books on Missional Communion

Sabbath, by Dan Allender

Sacred Rhythms: Arranging Our Lives for Spiritual Transformation, by Ruth Haley Barton

The Freedom of Simplicity, by Richard Foster

Books on Missional Engagement

God Next Door, by Simon Carey Holt

Rich Christians in an Age of Hunger, by Ronald Sider

The Coffee House Gospel, by Matthew Paul Turner

Books on Missional Relating

Caring Enough to Confront, by David Augsburger

Making Room for Life, by Randy Frazee

Relationships: A Mess Worth Making, by Tim Lane and Paul Trip

Books on Technical Leadership Skills

8 Habits of Effective Small Group Leaders, by Dave Earley

Community That Is Christian, by Julie Gorman

Finding the Flow, by Tara Miller and Jean Peppers

How to Lead a Great Small Group Meeting, by Joel Comiskey

Making Small Groups Work, by John Cloud and John Townsend

Simple Small Groups, by Bill Search

Practical Ideas That Can Be Used to Develop Missional Group Life

Small Group Idea Book, by Cindy Bunch

Small Group Ministry in the 21st Century, edited by Brad Lewis, with contributions from M. Scott Boren and sixteen others.

www.smallgroups.com

Note: While the ideas found in these books and on various websites were not written with missional small groups in mind, they can be applied and productively used to promote missional group life. The key is found not in the creative ideas but in the story the group lives. In other words, any of these ideas can be applied to missional groups living the story of Relational Revision as well as normal groups living the story of Lifestyle Adjustment.

Appendix C

The Role of a Pastor, Coach, or Elder in Developing Missional Small Groups

The best way for a group to play missional rhythms is to have three resources. First, they need the right instrument, which comes in the form of *each other*. Second, they need an introductory music book, which this resource aims to provide. Third, they need a missional music teacher who can help them process what they are learning and apply the rhythms in their context and to their specific church tradition.

If you are a pastor, coach, or elder who is supporting a group on a journey toward mission, please visit www.roxburghmissionalnet.com and download the free guide entitled "How to Support Missional Small Groups."

Notes

Chapter 1 A Different Drum

1. Paul Eddy, Unpublished Notes, Woodland Hills Church.

2. In *Introducing the Missional Church*, this is the second conversation topic. I changed the order of them in this book for the purposes of communicating the primary point that is being made in the chapters that follow. Alan J. Roxburgh and M. Scott Boren, *Introducing the Missional Church: What It Is, Why It Matters, How to Become One* (Grand Rapids: Baker, 2009).

Chapter 2 Rhythms of Everyday Life

1. Lesslie Newbigin, *The Other Side of 1984: Questions for the Churches* (Geneva, Switzerland: World Council of Churches, 1983), 5.

2. Randy Frazee, *Making Room for Life* (Grand Rapids: Zondervan, 2004).

3. Daniel Goleman, *Social Intelligence: The New Science of Human Relationships* (New York: Bantam Books, 2006), 10.

4. Ibid., 12.

Chapter 3 Listening to Your Small Group Story

1. These questions are a modification of the questions of an experimental church in the 1970s in West Houston. Ralph Neighbour Jr. writes about this in his book *The Seven Last Words of the Church* (Nashville: Broadman, 1973), 50.

2. Jean Vanier, *Community and Growth*, rev. ed. (New York: Paulist Press, 1989), 84–85.

Chapter 4 Relearning the Gospel Rhythms

1. Many might see this paragraph as a concession. I hope to write a book that addresses the strategic role that these groups play in moving people toward mis-

sional life. My book *The Relational Way* can help pastors and leaders understand the systemic differences that help promote missional (relational) life in groups.

Chapter 5 Three Basic Missional Rhythms

1. Some of these include Dallas Willard, *The Spirit of the Disciplines* (San Francisco: HarperOne, 1990); John Ortberg, *The Life You've Always Wanted* (Grand Rapids: Zondervan, 2002); Eugene Peterson, *The Jesus Way* (Grand Rapids: Eerdmans, 2007); Richard Foster, *The Celebration of Discipline* (San Francisco: Harper San Francisco: 1988); Brian McLaren, *Finding Our Way Again* (Nashville: Thomas Nelson, 2008); Dorothy Bass, *Practicing Our Faith: A Way of Life for a Searching People, Second Edition* (San Francisco: Jossey-Bass), 2010.

Chapter 6 The Rhythm of Missional Communion with God

1. Marva Dawn, *A Royal Waste of Time: The Splendor of Worshiping God and Being Church for the World* (Grand Rapids: Eerdmans, 1999), 1.

2. Ibid., 2.

3. Dave Earley and Rod Dempsey, *The Pocket Guide to Leading a Small Group: 52 Ways to Help You and Your Small Group Grow* (Houston: TOUCH Publications, 2007), 50.

4. See Scot McKnight, *Praying with the Church* (Brewster, MA: Paraclete Press, 2008).

5. Dietrich Bonhoeffer, *Life Together* (Minneapolis: Fortress Press, 1996), 82.

6. Ibid.

7. See the practical little book by Michael Mack, *The Pocket Guide to Burnout-Free Small Group Leadership* (Houston: TOUCH Publications, 2009).

8. Arthur Gish, *Beyond the Rat Race* (New Canaan, CT: Keats, 1973), 21.

9. Richard Foster, *Celebration of Discipline* (New York: HarperCollins, 1998), 80.

10. Ibid., 94.

11. Rita Finger, *Roman House Churches for Today: A Practical Guide for Small Groups*, second edition (Grand Rapids: Eerdmans, 2007), 157.

Chapter 7 The Rhythm of Missional Relating as a Group

1. Josiah Royce, *The Problem of Christianity*, vol. 2 (New York: Macmillan, 1913), 313.

2. Larry Crabb, *The Safest Place on Earth: Where People Connect and Are Forever Changed* (Nashville: Word, 1999), 32.

3. Dale Carnegie, *How to Win Friends and Influence People* (New York: Pocket Books, Simon and Schuster, 1964), 105.

4. Kathleen A. Brehony, *Living a Connected Life: Creating and Maintaining Relationships That Last* (New York: Henry Holt, 2003), 219–20.

5. Larry Crabb, *SoulTalk: Speaking with Power into the Lives of Others* (Brentwood, TN: Integrity Publishers, 2003), 28.

6. Ibid., 31.
7. Ibid., 231.

Chapter 8 The Rhythm of Missional Engagement with the Neighborhood

1. Howard Snyder, *Liberating the Church: The Ecology of Church and Kingdom* (Downers Grove, IL: InterVarsity, 1983), 53.

2. Parker Palmer, *A Hidden Wholeness: The Journey Toward an Undivided Life* (San Francisco: Jossey-Bass, 2004), 169.

3. Malcolm Duncan, *Kingdom Come: The Local Church as a Catalyst for Social Change* (Oxford: Monarch Books, 2007), 265.

4. Walter Brueggemann, *Interpretation and Obedience* (Minneapolis: Fortress, 1991), 294.

5. Christine Pohl, *Making Room: Recovering Hospitality as a Christian Tradition* (Grand Rapids: Eerdmans, 1999), 87.

6. Henri Nouwen, *Reaching Out: The Three Movements of the Spiritual Life* (Garden City, NY: Doubleday, 1975), 98.

7. Ibid., 99.

8. Mark Mittelberg of Willow Creek Community Church calls these Matthew Parties in honor of Matthew the tax collector.

9. It should be noted that a meal of the rich men in the village was not about friendship and mutual support. It was about social positioning. See Luke 14:7–10.

10. James F. Engel and Wilbert Norton, *What's Gone Wrong with the Harvest?* (Grand Rapids: Zondervan, 1975).

11. Wayne McDill, *Making Friends for Christ* (Nashville: Broadman, 1979), 6.

Chapter 9 Being Formed to Lead Missional Group Life

1. Alan Roxburgh, Fred Romanuk, Eddie Gibbs, *The Missional Leader: Equipping Your Church to Reach a Changing World* (San Francisco: Jossey-Bass, 2006).

2. See the research by Joel Comiskey, *Home Cell Group Explosion* (Houston, TX: TOUCH Publications, 1997).

3. All of the following quotes are taken from Elizabeth O'Connor, *Call to Commitment* (New York: Harper and Row, 1963), 86–91.

4. Ibid., 91.

5. This story is told in Stephen Pate and Gene Wilkes, *Evangelism Where You Live: Engaging Your Community* (St. Louis, MO: Chalice Press, 2008), 1–2.

M. Scott Boren is one of the pastors at Woodland Hills Church in Saint Paul, Minnesota. He is a trainer, a consultant, and the author of *Introducing the Missional Church* (with Alan Roxburgh), *The Relational Way*, and *How Do We Get There from Here?* He works with Roxburgh Missional Network as a consultant for churches who are seeking to move into missional patterns of life together and with Allelon in developing training materials on the missional church. He shares life with his bride, Shawna, and their four children.

ALLELON
A Movement of Missional Leaders

Allelon's mission is to **educate** and **encourage** the church to become a people among whom God can live, as sign, symbol, and foretaste of his redeeming love and grace in their neighborhoods and the whole of society—ordinary women and men endeavoring to participate in God's mission to reclaim and restore the whole of creation and to bear witness to the world of a new way of being human.

Visit **www.allelon.org** to read current missional thinkers, learn about our projects and resources, and more.

- Video and Audio of Leading Missional Thinkers and Practitioners
- Articles and Conversations
- Allelon Training Centers
- International Research Project: Mission in Western Culture

The word *allelon* is a common but overlooked New Testament word that is reciprocal in nature. Christian faith is not an individual matter. Everything in the life of the church is done *allelon*, for the sake of the world. A Christian community is defined by the *allelon* sayings in Scripture. We are to love one another. We are to pursue one another's good. We are to build up one another. We are to bear with one another in love. We are to bear one another's burdens. We are to be kind to one another. We are to be compassionate to one another. We are to be forgiving to one another. We are to submit to one another. We are to consider one another better than ourselves. We are to be devoted to one another in love. We are to live in harmony with one another.

Roxburgh Missional Network
catalyst for missional transformation

360s

Workshops

Webinars

Training

Coaching

Blog/Articles

How we address the issues of being the church today in the midst of huge culture change will shape us tomorrow. Becoming vital centers of mission in our communities no longer depends on categories we've taken for granted. The best practices of contemporary church life will no longer prepare us for the levels of change we face—we live in an *age of the unthinkable.*

The future of the church will depend on cultivating, discerning, and calling forth the unthinkable among the people of God in ordinary local churches.

Roxburgh Missional Network is a team of missional practitioners committed to partnering with you in forming leaders and churches that are vital centers of mission. We provide real-time, **concrete, hands-on resources** and **tools** that give pastors, denominational leaders, and congregations the capacities to address their challenges in forming mission-shaped communities. Our road-tested tools and resources are effective and cultivate mission-shaped transformation.

In an unthinkable world . . . it's all about the
CONVERSATIONS

www.roxburghmissionalnet.com

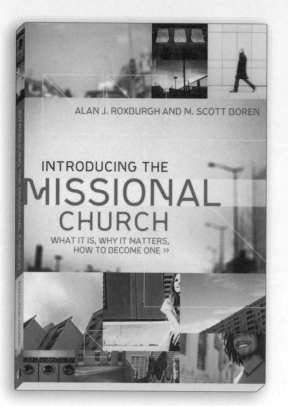

ALAN J. ROXBURGH AND M. SCOTT BOREN

INTRODUCING THE
MISSIONAL
CHURCH
WHAT IT IS, WHY IT MATTERS,
HOW TO BECOME ONE »

Introducing the Missional Church

WHAT IT IS, WHY IT MATTERS, HOW TO BECOME ONE

By Alan J. Roxburgh and M. Scott Boren

9780801072123
208 pp. • $17.99p

Many pastors and church leaders have heard the term "missional" but have only a vague idea of what it means, let alone why it might be important to them. But what does it actually mean? What does a missional church look like and how does it function? Two leading voices in the missional movement here provide an accessible introduction, showing readers how the movement developed, why it is important, and how churches can become more missional.

BakerBooks
a division of Baker Publishing Group
www.BakerBooks.com